BEYOND WORDS

BEYOND WORDS

Images from America's Concentration Camps

Deborah Gesensway
and Mindy Roseman

CORNELL UNIVERSITY PRESS   ITHACA AND LONDON

THIS BOOK HAS BEEN PUBLISHED WITH THE AID OF A GRANT FROM
THE HULL MEMORIAL PUBLICATION FUND OF CORNELL UNIVERSITY.

First published 1987 by Cornell University Press.
Second printing 1988.
First printing, Cornell Paperbacks, 1988.

Library of Congress Cataloging-in-Publication Data

Gesensway, Deborah, 1960–
  Beyond words.

  1. World War, 1939–1945—Concentration camps—United States. 2. Japanese Americans—History—20th
century. 3. Prisoners of war—United States—History 20th century. 4. Japanese Americans—Evacuation
and relocation, 1942–1945. 5. Prisoners as artists—United States. I. Roseman, Mindy, 1960–   . II. Title.
D805.U5G47   1987   940.54′72′73   86–29088
ISBN (cloth) 0–8014–1919–0 (alk. paper)   ISBN (paper) 0–8014–9522–9 (alk. paper)

Printed in the United States of America

*The paper in this book is acid-free and meets the guidelines
for permanence and durability of the Committee on Production
Guidelines for Book Longevity of the Council on Library Resources.*

TO OUR PARENTS

Contents

Preface

What was it like to be called "enemy alien" in the country of your birth, to prove your loyalty to the United States Constitution by giving up your constitutional rights? What was it like to be suddenly uprooted from everything familiar and corralled behind barbed wire for up to three years? These questions were vividly posed for us starting on an ordinary spring day in 1980, when we received separate phone calls from Richard Polenberg, a Cornell University professor of American history with whom we had taken a seminar in civil liberties. He told us that many boxes of papers and watercolors had just been discovered in an attic in Ithaca. The materials seemed to be from the World War II Japanese American relocation camps. Would we be interested in seeing them, that is to say, help carry the boxes to a place where they could be examined?

As we would later learn, these documents belonged to two former Cornell professors of anthropology/sociology—Alexander H. Leighton (also a psychiatrist) and Morris Opler—who had conducted sociological studies in two of the relocation camps, Poston (Arizona) and Manzanar (California). There were biographies, daily reports, minutes of meetings, and notes on all aspects of camp administration and life. But what particularly intrigued us was a series of 130 watercolors painted in Poston, Arizona, by one man— Gene Sogioka. These paintings, which ranged from landscapes to caricatures, were a visual record of the mass incarceration. As a collection, they conveyed a sense of what camp life was like, but individually the pictures were laden with ambiguity. It was not apparent that they were done in a concentration camp; there were no scenes of barbed wire and guard towers or other overt symbols of confinement. In many, Sogioka seemed to be sitting back and laughing about the whole situation—the humorous happen-

9

ings inevitable when five to eight people live in one 25-foot-square room and 250 people share one communal latrine. But in others, he seemed to be brooding over the great injustice done—the pictures evinced loneliness, despair, lack of hope for the future. It was as if Sogioka were challenging us: Draw your own conclusions. You figure out what it must have been like to be in our shoes.

Who was Gene Sogioka, the person behind the signature? What prompted him to paint these pictures, and what do they tell us more than forty years later? We thought that if we could locate him, he could help us answer some of these questions. And looking at his paintings we realized that other artists who had been interned might add to our understanding. They were people caught up in these events like other evacuees, but their experience as artists, we thought, might give them a unique perspective. Sogioka's watercolors spoke to us more vividly than any words could. Like photographs, they visually documented the events of the relocation, but with a deeper understanding, a more obvious personal touch. In order to paint a scene, an artist has to reflect on it, and those thoughts on and from the time remain fixed in the paintings. These paintings bear witness to an intensity that nearly forty-five years have otherwise mellowed.

In 1982 we began to search for other collections of concentration camp art. University archives and Japanese American organizations had some but not much. So we began detective work of our own. From camp documents we found names of people who had been involved in art in the camps. Then we thumbed through the nation's phonebooks and, to our surprise, located close to a third of our leads. Their reminiscences appear in this book. Much of their art has never been reproduced or shown before. These images are the product of America's concentration camps, the proof of what happened. Forty-five years later, the paintings tell us what the experience was like.

Initially, curiosity led us to these rich caches of art. But sustained excitement came when we heard the artists' stories, which not only described the paintings but gave us insight into how the artists themselves lived through the internment. In asking simple questions, we assumed we would get straightforward answers. But instead, how people felt about the camps was complex, or even ambivalent—adding dimensions to our understanding. The people with whom we spoke—and all the 110,000 people interned—went through the same ordeal but with different combinations of awareness and anxiety. Their unique experiences and perspectives, taken all together, are the meaning of the evacuation.

Our understanding of what it meant to have been confined behind barbed wire in our own country came from the twenty-five people we met and interviewed during the winter of 1982–83. (Short biographical sketches of them appear at the end of the book.) We wrote our book with the idea of

10

making the story of the evacuation come alive, complexity and all, through the people who had lived it. And that involves identifying with those people, with the many levels of consciousness that make up their experience.

We asked each person to tell us what he or she thought important. Certain elements emerged in all the interviews, which we took to be the themes of the experience. They provide the basis for four sections of the book. Here, paintings and drawings are interspersed with excerpts from many interviews to replicate the way the event was experienced. And to put these experiences in context, we added representative selections from the press and other sources.

The first chapter is called "Shikataganai," a Japanese word meaning "it can't be helped." It serves as an introduction, touching on all the themes and ideas that we later explore. The thematic chapters titled "Pioneer Communities" and "That Damned Fence" (Chapters 4 and 5) set the scene for Chapter 8, "The Sour and the Sweet"—the central theme of the book: what it was like to be interned. Chapter 11, the final thematic section of the book, is called "You Can't Black Out the Stars" and concerns the events following Pearl Harbor and leading up to the evacuation.

We have also included four individual narratives (Chapters 2, 6, 9, 12), believing that a few complete interviews will bring out the sense of the individual that might not be obvious in the theme sections. The four whom we chose, Henry Sugimoto, Miné Okubo, Kango Takamura, and Gene Sogioka, seemed to lend themselves to this kind of presentation. As well as having compelling stories, they had created distinctive paintings that comprehensively dealt with camp life. Each had been interned in a different camp, and all have followed careers as either commercial or fine artists.

Three chapters of political-historical narrative provide background and compensate for the gaps that result from interviewing a limited number and fairly homogeneous group of people. We have kept the narrative concise and germane to the thematic chapters that follow. Chapter 3 deals with the events between the signing of the exclusion order and the internees' arrival in camp. Chapter 7 confronts the issues of camp life. And Chapter 10 tells the story of the West Coast Japanese American community before the exclusion order and outlines possible explanations for the evacuation and incarceration.

The book is not organized chronologically. We chose to disregard this convention for reasons of emphasis. Our story is about the life the Japanese Americans lived in camp, not how they came to be there. To begin with the dramatic bombing of Pearl Harbor would be to overpower the everyday lived experiences of 110,000 human beings. The people with whom we spoke didn't remember the experience chronologically; rather they recollected anecdotes and expressed feelings. We decided to take our inspiration from them: we let their stories speak for themselves while largely suspending reference to the events that put them there.

The historical chapters are based on many accounts already written about the Japanese American relocation. Among these are: Roger Daniels, *Concentration Camps, North America*; Audrie Girdner and Anne Loftis, *The Great Betrayal*; Dorothy Swaine Thomas and Richard Nishimoto, *The Spoilage*; Dorothy Swaine Thomas, *The Salvage*; Frank Chuman, *The Bamboo People*; Michi Weglyn, *Years of Infamy*. We also drew upon the manuscript collections at Cornell University, the University of California at Berkeley and at Los Angeles, the Hoover Institution of War, Revolution, and Peace at Stanford University, the University of Arizona, and the National Archives.

We have employed terminology that has become conventional—the terms used by both government administrators and internees to soften the harsh reality. "Evacuation" refers to forced removal; a "project" is a camp. "Assembly centers" were temporary concentration camps; "relocation centers" were permanent concentration camps. We have used certain Japanese terms as well: "Issei" (first-generation immigrant, Japanese citizens at the time of World War II); "Nisei" (American-born, second generation); "Kibei" (American-born, educated, even partially, in Japan, returned to the United States); "Nikkei" (the ethnic Japanese community).

From the beginning of our project we were well aware of being outsiders —young and white, interviewing older ethnic Japanese. We did our best to convey our sincerity and break down the barriers, but inevitably we heard what we did because of who we are and who they are. And what we heard was how sensitive and resilient people made the best of, or survived in, or even prospered under adverse conditions. The artistic sensibilities of the people we interviewed contributed to their endurance. They could practice and teach their profession anywhere, while others—farmers and businessmen whose livelihoods were tied to a particular locale—could not. Artists had an opportunity to express themselves in their paintings, to comment on their situation, thereby gaining some control. Through art they could escape the confinement of camp; they could even briefly escape physically by going outside the barbed wire to paint. Many other internees were not as fortunate and are perhaps more bitter today.

We do not claim truth with a capital "t". The possible barriers to communication and the uniqueness of the group we interviewed, not to mention the nearly forty-five intervening years, cast shadows that to a point may obscure what happened. But shadows also add depth and detail; they help history correspond with life.

DEBORAH GESENSWAY AND MINDY ROSEMAN

Ithaca, New York

BEYOND WORDS

1

Shikataganai

Atsushi Kikuchi

The Japanese have a philosophy: "shikataganai"—"you can't help it." Things happen the way they happen, so live just day by day.

I was around twenty-three, twenty-four years old in camp. To keep my mind occupied I kept busy teaching and drawing. They were looking for some people with art training to conduct classes. I didn't mind teaching at all, except I never thought to do it as a profession. I had enough things to do so that I wouldn't be distracted by the misery of the experience.

I drew I don't know how many sketches. But before I was inducted into the army I got rid of everything I had. I had some drawings of the guard tower and barbed wire. Also of the surrounding town. There was a lot of community activity to unify the area, like digging trees to plant in camp; so I drew that type of thing. Also I played sarcastically with the evacuation—the short notice people got, when they had to dump everything on the street. Of Santa Anita, I played with the idea that people were housed in stables. . . . Whatever I could get a handle on, I'd scribble. I had many drawings of camp life, social conditions, political ideas, and so on.

Lili Sasaki

I don't think you can actually tell people how awful it was at that time, how terrible it was. And how embarrassing, because we thought we were being such good citizens and everything. It was a terrible state to be in, really. It was awful. Yes it was. We didn't know what to do. We didn't know what was going to happen because the Japanese were winning at that time —all along. They were going into the Philippines and they were winning,

15

Matsusaburo Hibi, Artists Painting in Camp (Topaz), watercolor.

you see. And I didn't want the Japanese to win. None of us did. We didn't want to be under Japanese rule, no.

The trouble was, we were all for Roosevelt. We voted for him. He was the best president we had in a long time. We didn't want to, but we said, "If that's what Roosevelt said, I'd be willing to go into camp. BUT, I don't like the Knights of Columbus or the American Legion telling us we want to kick the Japanese out of California." So what would you do? They had the gun and you had to go. We had no choice; we didn't like it. So when we got into camp, we wanted Roosevelt to take a stand and tell us what he intended to do with us. How come we're Americans and we had to go into camp? Why? While we were still in the internment camp at Santa Anita, why couldn't they go through us real fast and let us out, except those who wanted to go to Japan, instead of leaving us in so long? Why? Was it because they didn't have enough manpower? Or were they afraid Japan was going to come and invade California? Maybe that was it. We never did hear from Washington exactly where we stood.

Congressman John Rankin

Once a Jap, always a Jap. You can't any more regenerate a Jap than you can reverse the laws of nature.[1]

Justice Hugo Black

Our task would be simple, our duty clear, were this a case involving the imprisonment of a loyal citizen in a concentration camp because of racial prejudice. Regardless of the true nature of the assembly and relocation centers—and we deem it unjustifiable to call them concentration camps with all the ugly connotations this term implies—we are dealing specifically with nothing but an exclusion order. To cast this case into outlines of racial prejudice, without reference to the real military dangers which were presented, merely confuses the issue. Korematsu was not excluded from the Military Area because of hostility to him or his race. He was excluded because we are at war with the Japanese Empire, because the properly constituted military authorities feared an invasion of our West Coast and felt constrained to take proper security measures, because they decided that the military urgency of the situation demanded that all citizens of Japanese ancestry be segregated from the West Coast temporarily, and finally because Congress, reposing its confidence at this time of war in our military leaders, as inevitably it must, determined that they should have the power to do just this.[2]

Frank Kadowaki

But this concentration camp business is very bad. That means the mind always remains on what we did, on what passed in camp. And they made a big mistake. We didn't do nothing. We worked the same as the working people. We're working hard and pay the taxes and everything, same as other people. Only the Japanese-born didn't have citizenship. But the children born in this country, naturally, they were United States citizens. And my brother, he went to the 442nd and fought against the Germans. Even he went in the camp—and then he was drafted. . . . I think: forget it; forget it. Then always something happens and brings back a memory.

Lawrence Sasano

Obviously the whole thing was unbelievable. The whole thing was born of panic and fear. At that time, it was more a surprise than a question of whether it was justified or unjustified. You know that inevitably the truth would come out.

Earl Warren

Unfortunately [many] are of the opinion that because we have had no sabotage and no fifth column activities in this state . . . that means none have been planned for us. But I take the view that this is the most ominous sign in our whole situation. It convinces me more than perhaps any other factor that the sabotage that we are to get, the fifth column activities that we are to get, are timed just like Pearl Harbor was timed and just like the invasion of France, and of Denmark, and of Norway, and all of those other countries.

I believe that we are just being lulled into a false sense of security and that the only reason we haven't had disaster in California is because it has been timed for a different date. . . . Our day of reckoning is bound to come in that regard.[3]

Charles Mikami

I don't like to move, but I got a baby. And my wife got nervous breakdown right away. It was protection. Everybody was scared about Japanese submarines or disloyalty or something. Balloons with some kind of dynamite hanging came to Cascade Mountains and started forest fires. That happened two, three times. That's why America was scared. Japanese, maybe army, come. So protection. Better, all Japanese, American citizens or everything move.

> Army orders Japs to go to Parker Dam
> Sons of the sun never afraid of heat.
> They praise the burning rays
> And survive through the chaos.
> — Nyogen Sensaki[4]

Haruko Obata

We all agreed to follow the law. I don't think anyone protested it at that time. It was the law. Everybody just went along with it. The University people said [Chiura Obata] should go East, but he wanted to go with the rest of his people. He thought the people would need help, so he should go along. Friends in Salt Lake City had offered us their home and help in relocating East, but we decided to go to Tanforan. Partly because no cameras were allowed, he wanted to record all the events—everything that happened, every day.

> My aim is to create a bowl full of joy
> clear as the sky

pure as falling cherry petals
Without worry, without doubt;
Then comes full energy, endless power
And the road to art.
—Chiura Obata

Masao Yakubi

Obata asked me to help teach. . . . I had a classy job teaching kids. I ran the art department from seventh to twelfth grade; I had two assistants. They had their own classes, mostly seventh and eighth grades. What I taught, I told them: this is something you won't learn in high school. I'm teaching you as I was taught. The principle of drawing is "why." It's not how to draw; the main thing is "why." . . . I tried to explain to them the principles. I had some good teachers at Berkeley. I tried to teach them something.

19

Masao Yabuki, Tanforan Assembly Center Building a Pond (1942), opaque watercolor.

[We would draw scenes of Tanforan.] The barracks weren't quite ready then—built with green wood. Grass would sprout up between the cracks when the green wood dried. But the ones in the stables—just whitewashed and floor covering—couldn't get the smell out. . . . The smell! Can you picture this? You have to feel it to feel the situation. I'm drawing you a verbal picture.

Jack Matsuoka

I always wanted to draw ever since I can remember, I guess. I keep drawing and drawing. I carry a pen and brush with me wherever I go. But you have to consider the fact that my parents, they believed in hard work, and manual labor. My father worked as a launderer and my mother as a midwife. They believed you've got to work hard and save money—typical pio-

20

neer spirit. So in my case, I'd be drawing, thinking about some cartoons; to them, that's loafing. That's not exactly work. That's a lazy man's thing. My type of work didn't go over too well with them.

In camp I'd just sketch scenes that struck me. I'd get ideas—old timers just sitting around, something in their expressions. . . . I'd draw for my friends; that made me real popular. They'd hang around me. But I had no idea they were going to be a book. My mom saved the sketches [cartoons]. And then I exhibited them. Then a publisher grabbed them up.

Hisako Hibi

I am a painter, a very poor talker, very poor. Otherwise I would have been a writer. I have lived more than fifty years in the U.S., but do not yet speak English well. My Japanese is not good either. So please read between the words. We just talk with signs. When there is another painter and when we have feelings, we just put colors down. I can hardly believe today this kind of event happened. After forty-one years, it's so different. My mental condition is altogether different. After so many experiences . . . I don't know what to say. You cannot say in just a few lines what it was like.

Charles Mikami

I paint about three hundred pictures of camp scenery. At that time, we couldn't take a camera, take pictures. All swords, guns, and cameras prohibited. So I think I paint like I take a picture, you know. I have to put in the detail. So just the same as if I took it with a camera, these are.

Hiro Mizushima

I wish I had done more painting. I just did one drawing—a pencil sketch. It was in the camp. Actually it was outside the camp because I wanted to go outside. It was a little shack outside the camp, beyond the barbed wire. If I did paint, it would have been of the life of the people there.

George Akimoto

I did some sketching and drawing in my free time, but I don't have any now. Most of the people who sketched were either older people or the very introverted type who didn't socialize much. Normal people in their twenties would be out chasing girls instead of sitting around doing watercolors.

Nancy Sato

The only time my grandfather ever painted was in camp—never before and never after.

Yoriyuki Sato, Gila River Relocation Camp, watercolor.

Lawrence Sasano

I felt that with my background I could help young people, which I did. That made life easier for me. I kept busy with both high school and the young adults who wanted to learn fashion designing and art. The thing that hindered us in our artwork, or art teaching or production was lack of materials. That was a real challenge. We tried to get in touch with friends in L.A., elsewhere, to send us whatever objects they could get their hands on. And slowly we were able to get a few pieces of paper, a few pens, drawing ink, and a little coloring material.

Eiko Katayama

My father [Yonekichi Hosoi] would have died in camp if it weren't for his art. . . . He would just sit down and do these sketches in an hour. Without this, he would have died. . . . He was a free spirit who refused to be restricted

Yonekichi Hosoi, Topaz with Blackbirds, ink and brush.

and who loved to read philosophy. Many of his drawings depict scenes from Japanese stories drawn from memory. [Others] contain poetry and prayer.

If you look at these paintings, it seems like a vacation, but he saw only the good.

He was a pacifist who turned to art to escape the realities of war. He would ignore the sweltering heat, or his health, or forget to eat. He was an artistic type.

Matsusaburo Hibi

In the midst of this desert, we artists' job is not to discuss the war, nor waste time by gossiping and foment uneasiness among our residents. But our utmost efforts should be given to develop culture and soften the people's hearts which somehow seem to have a tendency to harden under the circumstances.

Existence of an art school now is more necessary and essential than ever before, especially in such a place as Topaz, where it is like a lone beautiful flower with a sweet fragrance in bloom. . . . It is not for the mere existence of teaching technique, but also to foster infinite inspirations, emotions, and peaceful thoughts in the people, young and old.[5]

Masao Mori

Before I came here from Japan, I was going to be an artist. I study; they have classes in high school. My father wanted me to come to the United States. I come in 1912. I like it. But I hear stories; good artists in the United States can't make a living. All kind of people heard stories like that. So I took a look. . . . Oh, I was so disappointed. Number one artists, they sell for 50 cents a picture. You can't live on that, so I was so disappointed. After that I put my pictures in frames and friends, neighbors see them and ask "how much for this?" I sell I don't know how many. I say, "You don't have to pay my price for my picture, but you have to pay me for my frame."

So what am I going to do for money? My relations have a florist shop in Berkeley—corner of University and Shattuck—good spot. I worked for him. There is art in flowers, you know, arranging flowers, so I like it.

Then in 1917 I start my own florist shop in Oakland. I was nineteen years old and they said I was too young yet. But I wanted to do the way I wanted. I made it pretty good. I bought a nursery, raised chrysanthemums, carnations. I didn't have time to sketch or draw though. In the florist shop, time is all tied up. In the morning you have to go buy flowers, worked all day decorating houses, weddings or something. All kinds of affairs. I did the best I could!

Los Angeles Examiner, 1943

One thing is certain, that war or no war, Californians will never again permit Japanese settlements in this state.

They were always contrary to the social development of American communities, they were economic menaces to American workers, wherever they gathered real estate values would decrease, their temples, schools, colonies, and slums were an offense and a danger.[6]

> Beyond those steel-blue western hills . . .
> California
> We huddle round the mesquite fire,

24

Yonekichi Hosoi, Topaz Art School, watercolor.

We old Isseis at sunrise,
In black coats,
Gazing . . .
Home.
Dreaming at sunrise, our eyes are big.
Why do our eyes become full?
>Do memories make eyes full?
>Does deep longing do this to eyes?
Only the western hill we see—no others,
Only the western hills have a glory,
>A glory wet and brimming.
Though their cold, steel blue shoulders blur as we gaze,
Only the western hills have magic.
Home.

—Anonymous[7]

Machiye Maxine Nakamura

There is no bitterness in me. . . . A sajuaro bloomed this spring, that queen of the desert, thriving stately where no nourishment is visible. It had this message to me that even in this seared land many things will bloom. One must stand above the sajuaro to see its beauty, so I too, must climb beyond the present difficulties, and search for that possible beauty that may come out of this thorny existence here.[8]

Atsushi Kikuchi

I never volunteer to talk about evacuation unless somebody asks about it. Not because of the experience, but because afterwards I felt it was a real miserable time. Perhaps it benefited the Japanese Americans in the sense that prior to the war they were concentrated in California, and a lot of the Japanese wouldn't mingle. Because of the evacuation, there was a chance for the Japanese Americans all over the United States. Now you can go any place and find Nisei. That probably would have never happened unless the relocation sent them out to the East and Midwest. I think it was good in that respect. Maybe the war would have done the same thing.

George Akimoto

Some of the younger kids around town get angry at us because they say, "Why didn't you protest?" like people do now. They don't know what they're talking about. In those days, you just didn't do things that way. Actually we just didn't have the time; it was a shock and you didn't have the time to sit

26

Masao Mori, Topaz through the Door, oil.

down and think about it. You just do what you're told and try to make the best of it.

I think we were forced into a situation and we weren't going to fight it. We just had to do the best we could in a bad situation.

Harry Yoshizumi

If you think back on it, then the impact hits. But that's in retrospect, so I don't know how relevant it is. You shut it out of your mind because you

Suiko Mikami, Topaz, August 1943, watercolor.

couldn't live with it, with that kind of traumatic experience. I think it was a bigger thing than we thought of then.

Los Angeles Evening Herald Express, 1943

America is being played for a sucker by the astute treacherous Japs who are being given their freedom to roam through war industry centers of the East and Mid-West by the War Relocation Authority. . . .

Have these government officials the minds of children? Have they forgotten the principles of those Japanese leaders who planned and executed the raid on Pearl Harbor even when their nation was supposedly on friendly terms with the United States? Do they believe for a minute that these internees at Manzanar and other camps intend to keep their word—that their word is worth anything?[9]

28

When there's a war, there's such a thing as war hysteria. And what people do at that moment might not have happened if they waited. Legally the evacuation is wrong; morally it's wrong. But to everything there are two sides and in a case like this, the majority has the upper hand. And the majority doesn't have to be right. Right? From this we have to be aware, and if possible, we have to try to not let this happen again.

Our parents have a word: "Shikataganai." It means: "Can't be helped." A thing has to happen the way it does. It just happens. And although I felt sometimes it could have happened some other way, I guess it was unavoidable. As I look back there was nothing we could do. We had no political power. And on top of that we were the easiest ones to pick on. Getting a minority that was different from the rest of the population—one-tenth of one percent—it's easy to see we're the ones that go into the camp.

2

Henry Sugimoto

Just now I can laugh, you know. Like dream. Yeah, like dream. So suddenly life changes, you know. Feels so bad. I don't know future—how many years this life in camp continues. That's why I was very worried.

Some people are so bitter. I am, of course, so worried and anxious that I was going to camp. So worried. But when I went to camp, I'm rather happy, you know, because I can do my work and do what I like. If I can still make my art, I am feeling not so bitter. I'm artist, and I can do my work any place, anywhere. Other people have quite a different feeling; that's just my feeling.

He was waiting outside on the stoop of his Harlem home in September 1982. Wearing a beret, well-worn blue jeans, a Cornell University windbreaker, and Keds, Henry Sugimoto waved to us: "I have to wait out here for you because the doorbell is broken. The neighborhood is so bad now." He folded up the newspaper he had been reading and ushered us into the lobby. "This used to be so beautiful . . . look at the mirrors, all broken now. And they stole all the furniture. Such a pity." He unlocked the door to his apartment. "Please come in, sit down, I'll be back in a minute." And so this gentle, spirited, and thoughtful man went into another room. Eighty some-odd years of life's vicissitudes have not daunted Sugimoto. He still cares and he still feels.

He returned with a copy of the book recently published in Japan of his camplife paintings. He has donated most of them to the museum in his hometown of Wakayama, Japan, because "they care about it over there. They are so interested." Around us, covering the livingroom walls, are large paintings from his latest project—recording the history of Japanese immi-

30

Henry Sugimoto, My Papa, oil.

gration to the United States. As he sets out a card table for our tape recorder, he says, "It's so nice you are interested. I'll tell you my story."

At the time of [Pearl Harbor] I was living in Hanford—large Nisei community, the parents made a Japanese-language school. So while I was staying there, they want me to help teach temporarily. So I took a teacher's position, just part-time work. In 1941—I am doing artwork and teaching Japanese —war broke out. Because I was teaching part-time in Japanese school, I am blacklisted with FBI. If I do my artwork, I have no trouble, but even a few hours a day teaching Japanese, maybe FBI look at me. I am so scared. If I were picked up by FBI, I can't see my family anymore. The people picked up by FBI, they put in jail most time; nobody can see any family. So I am worrying.

Japanese Buddhist Church reverend called: I am blacklisted. I had a Hanford High School classmate, he was assistant district attorney, so I contacted him. He said, "You close Japanese school first. When time comes, maybe you can open your school, but for a little while, you have to close it." I'm scared that any time I can be picked up, so I can't stay home painting anymore. I put fifteen dollars in my belt because they say if you are picked up by FBI only fifteen dollars you can carry. I got suitcases ready—heavy underwear—I don't know where we are sent, maybe north, maybe Montana, where it's cold.

A funny story here, a very pity story: a Japanese farmer, single, is scared to go outside. So this farmer is staying home when a peddler selling seeds came by. This farmer, old man, brought suitcase all ready, standing all ready to be picked up by FBI. The Caucasian peddler said, "This is not FBI, don't worry." I'm so pity for the farmer, you know. I painted a small one of FBI picking up a farmer without reason. And the wife cry and the baby is far away.

I was so nervous I could not paint any longer at home. My Japanese neighbor who worked on a ranch took me to work with him. That's better than staying home and being nervous. Our work there was pruning grape vines. I never had such an experience before. They taught me how to prune the vines. I worked slowly but . . . I tried my best but . . . I am so sorry, my line of grapes never got roots because I cut everything off. But every day I was able to forget about the FBI. I didn't want the money, just if I stay home, so nervous. I just kill time. War start, mostly you can't do anything in business. Soon the evacuation notice came.

The notice said you can't take anything, just clothes and eating stuff. Fork all right, but not sharp knife, you can't take it. And radio, you can't take it. My wife's parents had owned house; they built it. So we put all the stuff in the house, and I thought I might lock it up. But I asked a high school classmate, "You keep our house? If you want to rent to someone, rent it free, it's just that we want to keep house, you know." So this classmate, he had own house, so he let other poor people, without house, move in our house. But these people all take my things away. My material, lumber, tools and everything, even trunks—you know we lock up trunks—all open and my wife's beautiful kimono from our wedding, they all took them away. But I don't say anything, because embarrass my friend, you know. I thought responsible people he'd let use my house, but they took my stuff away.

That's why they ask for redress, you know. Some people quit their jobs; you had to quit job, you know. And everything taken. In the camp, under

Henry Sugimoto, Bewilderment, oil.

two thousand dollars you can claim. I lost all my hundred paintings left in gallery. A hundred paintings all gone. And after the camp closed I wrote letter. Letter came back. So I wrote my Caucasian friend: "Gallery already close one year ago." So I think they maybe auctioned my paintings. All gone. Four paintings came back that I left at Crocker Gallery in Sacramento. Everything else gone. But I only got a thousand dollars. It's worth more than ten thousand, but I want money at that time, need money, so two thousand all right. So I claim two thousand and government cut in half, so I got a thousand. But I gave lawyer the thousand, so left me just a few dollars, you know.

First time we're going to camp we made—you know Japanese people for picnic make rice ball or sushi—we made rice balls in case we missed lunch or something in the camp. And after we ate those rice balls, my daughter, still young—you know, five years old—don't know anything. She doesn't know what's happening, maybe it's a picnic. So we ate for lunch the rice balls. She said, "Let's go home. Already we ate all the rice balls." It's a picnic, you see! Can't even explain; they don't know. They can't understand it.

Cow and horse stable, that's how our families' living. Summertime, smell bad, you know, can't stand it. Only cool place—ten or twenty fig trees. That's only shading, so we get together over there—recreation. I painted there too. Anyway, we stayed about half the year, four to five months of this, in this Fresno camp.

34

During the few months in the assembly center, we all organize the young people. I teach art. Different people have different skills, so they teach each other, teach to those other people, to kill time. Then the government notice: We are moving to Arkansas, Jerome camp. We heard many rumors: In Arkansas, big rattlesnakes and so many rattlesnakes, and so many mosquitos like sparrows. If those mosquitos bite you, it sucks all your blood! Different scary rumors going around in the camp.

Then we entered the big train, just the one seat for three. I made the suitcase and clothes bundle for my daughter to sleep on. We squeeze like this —ten days—I don't know how many days we stayed. We can't count, you know. Black shade in the train and can't see outside. Can't see from outside how much time we passed. Sometime stop, you know, fifteen to twenty minutes to take fresh air—suppertime and in desert, in middle of state. Already before we get out of train, army machine guns lined up toward us— not toward other side to protect us, but like enemy, pointed machine guns toward us. So we can go in just a narrow place along the train. Just for a stretch, you know. Train slow and big noise. Already a toilet broke; floor all water, our belongings all wet. We had a hard time. Well anyway, I don't know how many days. One day I rode and already tired out, but maybe we rode for ten days. We arrived at McGhee, Arkansas.

But first we move in relocation camp, it was not quite ready. We had to stay one or two nights in a warehouse, right after the train. Warehouse—no beds, anything. We spread on the ground. They want small babies and sick people and very old people first ones to get ready barracks. Then after a couple of days, they gave us our room.

We're put in the same quarter—three, four people, one room. We go in, and there was nothing. Just a bed and mattress already filled and a blanket and a big stove for wintertime to make warm, you know. But we made ourselves furniture. I made a small table and bench. All families made it because mountain of scrap lumber outside the barrack. People pick up outside, make what they want to make. We shared the tools.

Japanese mostly rice eaters. So that's why WRA [War Relocation Authority] everyday cook rice—lot of rice—that help us. Mess hall's not like restaurant; if you refuse [to eat], you have to go hungry. But young people, you know, they want to eat a lot. At the first siren, young people come and eat. Then next mess hall, they go there and eat, because they can't get enough to eat. We are not so young, so we had enough. But rice, always rice. But pity thing—young kids, they don't have any sweets, candy. So parents made canteen. Otherwise, no sweets.

I brought a few tubes of pigment, three brushes, and a small bottle of tur-

pentine. But I don't have any canvas, no paper. So I use my sheets and pillow case and mattress. That mattress bag I took with me fortunately from the assembly center, so I started to paint. Whenever I could get heavy cotton sheets—that's canvas—I started to stretch it and I started to paint. First time I am scared. Maybe FBI look at me painting, and I will be taken away. So I set up inside. Very secretly I painted. I hide, working in my room because they don't come in our barracks, in our rooms.

One time an army lieutenant came to my place and said, "I want to take your picture inside your apartment." Perhaps on the outside they already heard I am artist, painting inside. So he came in: "I want to take your apartment picture." Inside I got paintings, still I'm painting, you know. That's why he told me: "We want to take movies. You do your work. Your wife bring to you some tea." Me, my wife—like actors. I am painting. My wife bring tea; serving the tea. Then they took movie. Then they took another movie in the mess hall. We went to lunch. On the corner table, so much food, chicken and all, like we never eat before here. They let them film to make record, you know. I ask lieutenant, "What are you going to do with those movies you took at my place?"

"That's only government record. In case it's needed, maybe they show it—we treat Japanese like this: artist, some people teaching school—very free and happy." That's our government record. That's why they let me act like that.

So I was free to paint. And the same time I taught in high school, so I have to requisition material for school work, paper and paint and watercolor. I put the material I need in with the other requisitions. They even sent me oil paint. They don't use in high school oil paint, but they give me. I made requisition for my work. So that's how I got canvas—very inferior, but anyway I got canvas. That's why I started all the paintings. The government gave to me. That's why now after forty years, some places already torn, but I mended. I keep it preserved.

Because in the camp, you know, no good scenery, just barracks, that's all—that's why naturally I take as subjects children, farmer going to farm, you know, the everyday life. We can go outside; I can paint outside the scenery. I have twenty to twenty-five outside-the-scene pictures. But mostly I concentrated on painting for a record. When I exhibit in Japan, I wrote in the catalogue: these paintings I painted just as it was. I don't want you to use as political propaganda. Don't use my paintings for that, but just as a record of Japanese actions and doings in the camp.

One day, two Hendrix College [Arkansas] art professors came to visit me, Japanese artist in camp. So I show my paintings. That time already I had fifteen—more than fifteen—paintings already. And I show them everything. And they said, "Oh, that's wonderful. We want to exhibit you a one-man show at the college." So I had to ask the director for permission. He said, "That's very nice." Sometimes, director took my three, four paintings to show for public relations. So the director said, "Very nice; good chance." So they exhibited me in Arkansas, Hendrix College museum. They have a small museum. They took maybe a dozen or more paintings which I had painted already. Nineteen forty-two, end of year, that's when I exhibited there. There were mostly students; the public was invited, but mostly students and professors. But two professors came to me and said, "Mr. Sugimoto, you're doing very nicely. This is very important for you and for the Japanese people, for a record." At that time, I was told: "You make record. Paint as many as you can." So I decided really I have to make a record. So I started mostly those documentary paintings.

John Gould Fletcher—Pulitzer Prize winner—saw my paintings. A very kind letter came to me in camp. He wrote me a letter: "*Longing* very much impressed me, so from this your painting I made my poem." I met later Mr. John Gould Fletcher.

Then my friend gave me some big sheets: "If you paint, I give to you." So about fifteen of those big sheets I've got. That's all coarse, not primed, ordinary cloth, very hard to paint, you know. Anyway, that's how I painted fifteen quite large. During the stay in camp I made fifty small and big size. After they closed Jerome camp, the Rohwer camp high school invited me to "come over to my school; I want you to teach art." So my family moved to Rohwer and stayed there until nearly the camp closed, about ten to fifteen days before because when the camp was closing I wanted to paint it. But they told me, "Mr. Sugimoto, you have to go out now, otherwise you have to carry home your baggage yourself."

At that time, I got appendicitis, so friend of mine, doctor, looked at me. "Oh, it's your appendix, you better have operation. I'll operate on you. Because if you go outside, a thousand dollars you'll have to spend; I'll operate right here." So he operated on me fifteen days before we leave.

So then we left camp for New York. A minister—he was commissioned to visit camp to camp—when he came to visit my camp, he always came to see me. And he said, "Mr. Sugimoto, where do you want to go? You want to go back to California?" And I said, "No, I am artist. If I can, I want New York." That's best, because New York not so much discrimination. Before the war, we had so much discrimination. So mostly, people go to New York or Chicago—they're all spreading after the war, all spreading.

Henry Sugimoto, Longing (1944), oil.

For the Picture "Longing" of Henry Sugimoto

Though the snake—hiss
Casts its menace, and the train roars off through cloud
Lightning fanged beyond these towns, there is yet no higher bliss
Than what rests above the present terror of this flood;
Mother love, sad with presage, yet accepting all.
Lacking this, we would be nothing, and our fall
into the pit would be endless—with this, we may crawl
Out of hopeless Longing, make new heaven out of hell
Here where we hold to this purpose, here where we dwell
We may walk the earth yet—broken, yes—but watchful still and proud.

—John Gould Fletcher

3

History I: Executive Order 9066

On February 19, 1942, under the guise of "military necessity," President Franklin D. Roosevelt signed Executive Order 9066, providing for the mass evacuation and incarceration of Japanese and Japanese Americans. In March 1942, General John L. DeWitt, head of the Western Defense Command, ordered all people of Japanese descent out of militarily sensitive areas along the Pacific. DeWitt divided the states of Washington, Oregon, California, and Arizona into two military areas and grouped Idaho, Montana, Nevada, and Utah into a third. Between March 2 and March 24, he ordered Japanese residents to leave Military Area 1 (the western half of the West Coast states and Arizona). They could resettle in Military Areas 2 and 3, or elsewhere in the country if they desired. For those displaced Japanese Americans who did not have the resources for such a move, the military set up assembly centers to accommodate them until they could find a way to move to the free zones inland.

Of the approximately 127,000 people of Japanese ancestry in the United States in 1940, about 113,000 of whom lived in the West Coast states, nearly 80,000 were American citizens, most of them under twenty-five. The rest were Issei who (except for World War I veterans) were barred by federal statute from naturalizing. Together they comprised .09 percent of total U.S. population, 1 percent of the West Coast's—hardly a threat. But they were less assimilated than other groups of immigrants by virtue of their culture and appearance. The Japanese immigrants were mostly poor, but not destitute, farmers and fishermen who were hard-working and proud. The first generation did their best to make better lives for their families—just as had German and Italian immigrants, who comprised much larger percentages of the population.

Most of the older and more experienced community leaders (almost entirely Issei men) had been arrested in the immediate aftermath of Pearl Harbor and spent the first part of the war in Department of Justice detention camps.

A policy of forced internment for all other West Coast Japanese Americans became a reality after the Tolan Committee (a congressional committee headed by Representative John H. Tolan of California) surveyed the intermountain states for possible voluntary resettlement sites for the Japanese American community. It found that all the governors except Ralph Carr of Colorado refused to permit the West Coast Japanese into their states except under armed guard and behind barbed wire. It was the Tolan Committee that recommended the "immediate evacuation of all persons of Japanese lineage" and called for the creation of a federal agency to oversee their removal and establish concentration camps. The hysterical reaction of the mountain state governors was by no means unique. Military Area 2—composed of the eastern halves of California, Oregon, and Washington, and supposedly a sanctuary for the already resettled Japanese Americans— became a hunting ground for fanatical "Jap" haters. War in the South Pacific became war against these relocated people. Violence against the Japanese American community gave rise to a new rationale for total evacuation; the "it's for their own protection" argument joined the battery of reasons to incarcerate an entire ethnic group of people regardless of citizenship. Area 2 was ordered evacuated.

In March 1942, after receiving various recommendations, President Roosevelt issued another executive order establishing the War Relocation Authority (WRA), a civilian agency to administer the militarily prompted evacuation and internment. Milton S. Eisenhower, then a Department of Agriculture official, reluctantly assumed leadership, to be replaced later that summer by Dillon S. Myer, also of the Department of Agriculture. The policy of the WRA as stated in April 1942 had three aims: to establish government-sponsored centers in which some of the evacuees could be quartered and could work on government projects to pay for their support; to oversee resettlement elsewhere; and to support agricultural pioneer colonies. Although WRA policies changed during the course of implementation, their real thrust remained the same: to set up detention centers to house people who were thought to be disloyal and perhaps dangerous. The "military necessity" that had in February demanded evacuating a region now required incarcerating people accused of nothing but being Japanese in ancestry.

The army agreed to construct the WRA's detention centers. They would be built on unused federal land; that is, on land so desolate and forbidding that no one had wanted or tried to develop it. Ethnic Japanese were evacuated from all the designated areas and transported to fifteen assembly centers—Fresno, Marysville, Merced, Pinedale, Pomona, Salinas, Santa Anita, Stockton, Tanforan, Tulare, Turlock, and Walerga, in California; Portland, Oregon; Puyallup, Washington; and Mayer, Arizona. These temporary detention camps were mostly hastily converted fairgrounds, racetracks, and livestock exhibition halls. Each held approximately 5,000 people except Santa Anita, which held more than 18,000, and Mayer, which held only 247. People were also being moved into Manzanar, California, and Poston, Arizona, two of the permanent relocation camps; they housed evacuees even before they were completed. At the peak of the evacuation, 3,750 people a day were being moved.

Nobody wanted to go, but except for a few isolated cases, the evacuation went "without mischance, with minimum hardship, and almost without incident," according to Colonel Karl Bendetson, one of DeWitt's assistants. But resentment was there, if concealed. Almost everyone lost monetarily and otherwise. Loss of pride and even of faith in democracy was apparent. The Japanese American Citizens League (JACL), a Nisei social organization that the war had pushed to a position of political leadership, had repeatedly proclaimed its loyalty to America. Since the members' protestations were ignored, it seemed the only way to demonstrate their patriotism was to comply with the government's orders. To disobey, ironically, would be to show disloyalty.

The WRA defined an assembly center as "a convenient gathering point, within the military area, where evacuees live temporarily while awaiting the opportunity for orderly, planned movement to a relocation center outside of the military area." Although assured by officials and the press that these temporary homes were by no means "concentration camps," the Japanese American refugees discovered on arrival that they were not merely surrounded by barbed wire fences, but were also policed from guard towers by armed soldiers. Inside the fence, conditions were worse than most ever expected. A quick coat of paint and some linoleum made animal stables into apartments. Without regard for health or safety, let alone aesthetics, the army slapped up shoddy barracks for latrines, mess halls, and additional housing. The only requirement of their construction was that they be made available for occupancy. For three to six months, while the more permanent relocation centers further inland were being planned and then built, about 10,000 people lived within the camps at these gathering points.

The move to permanent relocation centers began in the summer of 1942, and by November the transfer was complete. The evacuees boarded decrepit, sluggish trains, the only ones not transporting troops or other war support materials. Their journeys lasted up to ten days. Black shades covered the train windows day and night. The trains stopped at regular intervals in areas far from cities or stations to let the travel-weary captives stretch. Their movement was restricted to a narrow strip alongside the train by armed guards, who aimed guns at the Japanese Americans. Disoriented and exhausted, the evacuees arrived at their new homes.

There were ten relocation centers, each of which housed 10,000 to 20,000 Japanese Americans. They were: Manzanar and Tule Lake, California; the Colorado River Relocation Project (Poston) and Gila River, Arizona; Jerome and Rohwer, Arkansas; Heart Mountain, Wyoming; Central Utah (Topaz); Minidoka, Idaho; and Granada (Amache), Colorado. The WRA defined a relocation center as "a pioneer community, with basic housing and protective services provided by the Federal Government, for occupancy by the evacuees for the duration of the war."[1] A later WRA pamphlet encouraging internees to relocate out of the centers offered a less sanguine, but more telling description: "Relocation centers, by their very nature, can never be turned into normal communities in the full sense of the phrase; they will always have serious shortcomings."[2]

An evacuee's first view of his or her wartime home encompassed monotonous rows of dreary black tar-papered barracks often surrounded by barbed wire and usually twenty or thirty miles from the nearest small town. The ten relocation camps were located in deserts and swamps, the most desolate, hostile areas of the country. Their extreme weather conditions were a tremendous shock to the refugees, most of whom had spent their lives in temperate California. The physical conditions of the camps and their environs were to affect daily life perhaps more than anything else, and have remained the most vivid aspect of the internees' memories more than forty years later.

4

Pioneer Communities

Lili Sasaki

When we got there [Amache, Colorado], everybody was shocked because there was nothing but sand and sandstorms and tumbleweeds. Not a thing to see. We would just get so bored that when the sun went down after dinner, we all put our arms around each other and kept running up and down these long lanes, singing songs. I remember skipping, acting silly. That's what we did. So whenever I hear these old songs it reminds me of camp.

The worst part was these sandstorms that we weren't accustomed to. A lot of the Japanese never saw a cold day in their life, growing up in California. They didn't know what that black rock was for—it burns—that was a surprise. But then it used to get so cold; by the time you walk over from the shower to your little barrack room, your towel is stiff. They told us since the temperature could fall so suddenly you could get frozen to death. Within twenty minutes it could fall to 20 below. It was too dangerous to go outside. Yes, it did get that cold. It was a surprise to us. We had to keep the fire burning all the time.

And then the dust storm came. I remember my daughter disappeared once and I couldn't find her and her little friend. I looked for them all over. There was a very religious young pastor—evangelist type—and I looked in his church and I could hardly see, the sand was so bad. And I looked in and there I saw my little daughter and her girlfriend right in the front row. And I thought what in the name of the world brought them there, because I lived way on the other side of the camp. I heard him say, "You know when you get to heaven you're not going to have all this dust." Finally I got my daughter. It was so bad that we didn't know how to act . . .

45

Chiura Obata, Topaz Duststorm (August 1945), watercolor.

Masao Mori
The weather was much different than Oakland. A lot of snow; and summertime, oh, hot and storms. . . . I have those sketches too—of tornados and winds . . .

War Relocation Authority Pamphlet
Be prepared for the Relocation Center, which is a pioneer community. So bring clothes suited to pioneer life and in keeping with the climate or climates likely to be involved. . . . Bring warm clothing even if you are going to a southern area, because the temperatures may range from freezing in winter to 115 degrees during some periods of the summer.[1]

Can this hard earth break wide
The stiff stillness of snow

46

And yield me promise that
    This is not always so?

Surely, the warmth of sun
    Can pierce the earth ice-bound
Until grass comes to life
    Outwitting barren ground!
          —Toyo Suyemoto[2]

Frank Kadowaki

   In camp, well we had a very sorrowing time. It was very bad. Because in the building, the floor had space between the boards. You know Poston is the desert. Desert with big winds blowing. The wind is blowing. All of a sudden—vroom, vroom—just like a tornado. The sand blows right under

47

the house, then goes into the room. Even when we sit about three feet apart, you could hardly see each other's face. Oh, that was terrible. We used a handkerchief on the mouth to breathe. Oh, it was terrible at that time. But six months later we decided to start growing something around the area; we planted alfalfa between the barracks. . . . That helped the blowing dust. That had quite a bit of control.

Atsushi Kikuchi

Granada, Colorado. They used to call it a sand bowl, I think. Whenever they had a wind, the whole place filled up with dust. It was almost like a fog. And that was a reason why on the weekends people went outside to find some trees along the river. Volunteers got together, went out, dug trees, and planted them around the barracks. And then most of the people, since there wasn't much to do, started vegetable as well as flower gardens. By the time I left, it was quite green. Wasn't that much of a sand storm after that. And the buildings were more or less built temporary, like barracks, you know, no insulation or anything like that.

We didn't have any deep snow, but I remember one year we had snow in the morning and it was around the edges of the barracks where the foundation was. I remember snow inside the houses about four to five inches. Let's see, I think we had lowest temperature about 25 below one day. So it could get pretty cold. And in the dry climate, you could really feel the cold. Plus that wind factor. And I was located in just about the end corner of the camp, and the school where I taught was at the other end. A lot of people had frozen noses, ears from that cold weather.

There was a small village just outside of camp; I don't remember about how many houses. It was a small place, about ten miles west. It was the closest town. Except for one village the camp was right in the middle of the desert, nothing. There was sagebrush and cactus . . . a very barren place.

Masao Yabuki

When we got there [Topaz, Utah] it was only barracks. They hadn't finished the road yet and it was dusty. It was beyond words. The main road was graveled. The others were just clay—like flour. You step on it—phew! The wind would blow, come through the cracks. They gave us one army blanket—you know, khaki—it turned out to be cream-colored because of the dust.

Hiro Mizushima

The barrack itself was just tar paper on the outside. We had a pot belly stove; Arkansas did get pretty cold. The inside was just bare wood walls and there were cots, just like army cots. The floor was just bare. I remember air coming through the bottom. But I have to give the Issei and the Japanese people a lot of credit because they did something with it. Even these dull-looking black tar paper covered barracks became attractive after a time. They put gardens in front of them and all that. Rohwer was in a wooded area and it was quite nice. So it wasn't as bad as people might think and still it wasn't as good.

> Mountains, mountains!
> Wait until the days
> In which you can see
> The old peaceful America again.
> —Nyogen Sensaki[3]

49

Harry Yoshizumi, Poston Mess Hall, watercolor.

Kakunen Tsuruoka, Poston, Arizona Landscape, watercolor.

Estelle Ishigo, Heart Mountain, Wyoming, watercolor.

Matsusaburo Hibi

Whirlwind of World War forced us, 8,000 men, women, and children three years ago right into the midst of Utah desert, where there was one mile square surrounded with barbed wires. All we could see then, there were infinite sky, mountains miles away, and southern horizontal line across the vast broad sage brushes. . . . Nothing but dwelling places of rabbits, coyotes, snakes, and scorpions.[4]

Mountains laying around Topaz are all too far away to reach by human legs; however, every once in a while, we can take trips to mountain by car, where there are only a very few low trees are growing. The surroundings are very lonesome and somewhat look like a dead old battle field. When we can find a little green grass in our living Center, it looks to us as if a green diamond. In another word, everything is dried up and gray-colored in this plateau; it seems even so in our evacuees' hearts too.[5]

Yoriyuki Sato, Gila River Relocation Center, watercolor.

Lawrence Sasano

If you went to an area without any trees, totally barren and full of silt knee-high, and if you went into this all by yourself—nothing but silt around you—it would be a very discouraging environment, right? Well, this is the kind of environment they selected. This [Poston, Arizona] is Indian reservation, but none of the Indians wanted it! Just barren, worse than desert, it's nothing but silt, knee-high. Just picture those barracks in that silt. Weather-wise, I took it as it came. Dusty, stormy days where the only place you could be was in your room in the barracks, and even the barrack was no haven because all that silt was blown in. You'd see a black cloud in the distance and that meant you take cover. And all that silt came right through the fine cracks. And when it was over, probably in about forty minutes, your bed, all your clothing was just covered with silt.

So when we were stuck in this desert, it was a challenge, but it just fit in my pattern, see. Everything is a challenge.

53

Kakunen Tsuruoka, Mesquite at Poston, Arizona, watercolor.

Chiura Obata, Topaz at Night (1944), watercolor.

Like we didn't have any stoves at first. In the wintertime, I used to get mesquite wood and build a fire for about an hour so it turns to coal. Then I dig a trench in the sand, cover it with sand, and sleep over it. Nice and comfortable.

I would go to the desert myself, alone. I would bring back cactus plants, fourteen-foot cactus—to plant an exotic cactus and water garden. There was another reason I went to the desert: to prospect for wood. Buried for hundreds of years in the river washes are pieces of wood, maybe just a tip like that is sticking out. It's not what you call petrified, but had enough silica in it, through immersion in the sand and water, that the coloration had changed to a deep purple and orange, red, yellow in the wood. I used to do that—just be able to spot those things sticking out in the sand, dig them out, and bring them home to camp.

Masao Mori, Topaz Landscape, oil.

Haruko Obata

It [Topaz] was a totally different environment from what we were used to in Berkeley—dry and hot. There were scorpions, too. We never had seen those before. The sunsets were beautiful, though. Everybody was always complaining, but Chiura would say, "Just look around."

Anonymous

Mr. M. Y., as he was sitting on his porch and looking at the horizon, was amazed to find that he had missed so much the beauty of nature. Being so occupied before, he had not been able to appreciate the beauty of a sunset. Now he wishes he had learned to express himself with a pen or a brush.[6]

Hisako Hibi

Here too I felt sad—heaven and earth, everything seemed gray. I used lots of gray color . . . although the nature was always beautiful! The desert sunrise and sunset, so brilliant and so magnificent, somehow I could not bring out the brilliant colors on the canvas. The stars at night were another beauty, clean and clear. On a clear night in camp—moonrise—you forget everything. Really forget everything.

5

That Damned Fence

Of the first group of West Coast Japanese Americans evacuated, only a portion found their new homes fenced in. The desolate environment of desert sand and mountains was considered barrier enough. But for puzzling reasons, the WRA and the army decided to erect barbed wire fences around the open camps. Residents watched themselves being fenced in, and in some camps helped to build the fences. Protests were organized, but the fences, with guard towers manned by armed military patrols, for the most part, remained.

Lili Sasaki
I always thought to myself, "Would those GIs actually shoot my daughter if she happened to go near the fence?" I was almost tempted to say, "Go on there, Mimi. Go out there and pick that flower over there." See if the GIs. . . .

Shizuko Horiuchi
The life here cannot be expressed. Sometimes we are resigned to it, but when we see the barbed wire fences and the sentry tower with floodlights, it gives us a feeling of being prisoners in a "concentration camp." We try to be happy and yet, oftentimes, a gloominess does creep in. When I see the "I am an American" editorial and write-ups, the "equality of race" etc.—it seems to be mocking us in our faces.[1]

War Relocation Authority Report (1942)
A sentry at Manzanar shot full a 17–18 year old with buckshot because he went beyond the fence. The youth said he had permission.[2]

58

Estelle Ishigo, Children Flying a Kite (Heart Mountain 1944), watercolor.

Togo Tanaka
My constant and repeated reference to that fence is perhaps unfair because it seems to leave so little room for all the happy things that went on and continued to go on within the relocation camps. But these happened in spite of and not because of it.[3]

War Relocation Authority Report (1943)
[They] asked that something be done about the serious situation of ball players who go beyond the boundary to retrieve balls (also golf players), who if not properly warned, might be accidentally shot by guards who might suspect them of escaping.[4]

Haruko Obata
Every now and then students from Berkeley would come to visit their old

Chiura Obata, Tanforan (July 1942), pen and ink.

professor. They would say, "Oh, how terrible, Professor Obata, you are behind the fence!" And he would answer them by saying, "From my perspective, it looks like you are behind the fence!"

Block Manager's Log, Poston (1942)

Yesterday the residents of this block were informed by the surveyor that there will be a fence around the limits of this community. . . . I cannot face my own residents with a straight face. . . . Do you suppose we're going to escape? Or is it to keep out cows and horses? . . . And now we see the realities of a concentration camp. Even if it's for cattle, the very idea of placing a fence around the limits of this community is wrong. It is the principle of the whole idea. Should the wire be nailed on, the result will be that we are cattle and consequently the prisoners of war.[5]

Chiura Obata, Hatsuki Wakasa Shot by MP (Topaz, April 11, 1943), watercolor.

Haruko Obata

At the beginning an old man had befriended a little dog. The dog ran through the fence one day and that old man ran after the dog. The guard in the watchtower shouted a warning to him, but the old man couldn't hear him or couldn't understand the warning or something and was shot and killed. After that, they hung red warning signs on all the fences.

At parties, my husband used to ask a person from the audience to draw a stroke on a piece of paper, and he'd make a painting from it, and they could keep it. One day at a party at the administration building, he was doing the same thing. One woman said, you'll never be able to do anything with this, and she proceeded to draw a red square. So he looked at it for a long time, and then drew a beautiful sunset. He added barbed wire, and everyone

61

knew then that he had transformed the square into the red keep-away signs that were ruining the beautiful view from camp.

War Relocation Authority Report, Manzanar (1943)
The fence, the guards, the towers and their implications make a still deeper impression because, along the east boundary, the fence runs only a few feet from a main highway. This segment of highway lies between Independence, the county seat, and the town of Lone Pine. It connects this region with the more thickly populated area to the south. There is consequently a fair amount of traffic upon it, and the contrast between the barbed wire and the confinement within Manzanar and the observable freedom and motion for those immediately outside, is galling to a good many residents.[6]

George Akimoto
Soon after [we came to Rohwer], as a protest, about a half dozen of us got hold of a wire cutter, so we sneaked off into the outskirts to a wooded area of our camp. And we decided we were going to cut the barbed wire. One of the guys had glasses. We cut the wire, and the wire, you know because of the tension, sprang back and smacked him in the glasses. So we were groping around looking for the pieces of glass, because we didn't want the FBI to find them and identify them!

Hiro Mizushima
Then we went back to the paper and wrote that people shouldn't be doing things like that [cutting barbed wire]! I mean I can laugh about it now, but at the time, it was something serious. I thought we were doing something.

Dies Committee Report (1943)
At one camp the Japanese objected to a fence which confined them. They tore it down. It stayed down, and the Japs are still roaming around there at will.[7]

Dillon Myer
It is true that a section of the fence surrounding the Minidoka center has recently been removed and has not yet been replaced. . . . It was removed by evacuee labor crews working under orders of the War Relocation Authority and with the full knowledge and consent of the military authorities.[8]

62

Chiura Obata, Keep-Away Sign at Topaz (1943), watercolor.

Suiko Mikami, Topaz at Night (February 1944), watercolor.

Unidentified Minidoka Resident

The fence came down because people wanted to use it for a clothesline. Who was going to walk out in the middle of the desert? There was no reason at all for that barbed wire.[9]

That Damned Fence

They've sunk in posts deep into the ground,
They've strung wires all the way around.
With machine gun nests just over there,
And sentries and soldiers everywhere!

We're trapped like rats in a wired cage

To fret and fume with impotent rage;
Yonder whispers the lure of the night
But that DAMNED FENCE assails our sight.

We seek the softness of the midnight air,
But that DAMNED FENCE in the floodlight glare
Awakens unrest in our nocturnal quest,
And mockingly laughs with vicious jest.

With nowhere to go and nothing to do,
We feel terrible, lonesome, and blue;
That DAMNED FENCE is driving us crazy,
Destroying our youth and making us lazy.

Imprisoned in here for a long, long time,
We know we're punished though we've committed no crime
Our thoughts are gloomy and enthusiasm damp,
To be locked up in a concentration camp.

Loyalty we know and patriotism we feel,
To sacrifice our utmost was our ideal.
To fight for our country, and die, mayhap;
Yet we're here because we happen to be a Jap.

We all love life, and our country best,
Our misfortune's to be here in the west;
To keep us penned behind that DAMNED FENCE
Is someone's notion of National Defense!!!

—Anonymous[10]

6

Miné Okubo

We were suddenly uprooted—lost everything and treated like a prisoner with soldier guard, dumped behind barbed wire fence. We were in shock. You'd be in shock. You'd be bewildered. You'd be humiliated. You can't believe this is happening to you. To think this could happen in the United States. We were citizens. We did nothing. It was only because of our race. They did nothing to the Italians and the Germans. It was something that didn't have to happen. Imagine mass evacuating little children, mothers, and old people!

Miné Okubo, with long black hair pulled back, laugh-outlined eyes, a colorfully flowered shirt, and an energetic gait, opened the door of her Greenwich Village studio apartment to us in September 1982. "Well come on in, sit down, I must tell you I am very busy, so many things to do," she said before we could introduce ourselves. Creative, playful, even mischievous, Okubo has a puckish charm qualified by a seriousness of purpose gained through seventy years of experience—a commitment to bettering the human condition through universal and enduring truth in art, as she later explained. She shows and tells it straight, with an astringent wit. But for all her abruptness, Okubo is not harsh. The reassuring gleam in her eye betrays her basic belief that nothing could be all that bad.

I had always wanted to come out East, but I didn't know anybody and I was shy. So when the evacuation came, I said, "God has answered my prayers!" All my friends asked why don't I go East instead of going to camp. I said, "No, I'm going camping!"

At the time I was working for the WPA doing artwork—murals in mosaic and fresco for the army in Oakland. I was working in the daytime when Pearl Harbor was bombed. We were taken completely by surprise, but we thought the citizens wouldn't be evacuated.

There was a curfew from 8 P.M. to 6 A.M. I had to get a special permit from the government so I could go beyond the five-mile radius to go to Oakland for work. I worked and finished the murals a few days before the evacuation day.

My mother had died before evacuation, so my youngest brother came to live with me in Berkeley. Another brother was drafted in the army before Pearl Harbor. My father was living alone in Riverside. My sister came from Pomona to visit him one day and the whole house had been ransacked—everything we had, all the old Japanese suitcases filled with parents' old kimonos, my parents' past life. Everything had been stolen. Everything. It looked like he had been taking a bath and cooking when the FBI came to take him away. My sister made inquiries and found him in the Riverside jail. But they wouldn't let her see him. You see, anyone who was connected with any Japanese organization was considered potentially dangerous and when Mother died, Father started helping at the Japanese church. He was shipped to a [U.S. Department of Justice] camp in Missoula, Montana.

My brother and I were evacuated to Tanforan racetrack for six months and then to Topaz, Utah, for one and one-half years. I would get letters from my father. It would read: "Dear Miné, Block, block, block" [blocked out by the censor] and his name signed. So I never found out what happened. Then I received letters from Louisiana. It was the same: block, block, block, block. Finally I had a letter from him saying they were releasing him. That was while I was still in camp. They had cleared him. He decided to go to Heart Mountain to be with my sister and brother. But before evacuation he had met a widow in the Japanese church and she was in the Poston camp. Father was very lonely so I told him he should transfer. He did go there and they were finally married and eventually moved back to Japan. He died there.

In Tanforan, before we went to Utah, all those that had any business problems that they wanted to settle could get out for one day, with a guard. This poor fellow went out of his mind! I took him to the University of California. Met all the professors. And fed him at the faculty club. Bought lots of candy; we weren't allowed candies at that time. We just made it back to camp in time. It was crazy. I mean if you were guilty or something, fine. But it's a strange feeling to have a guard along. But everything was insane when you didn't do anything. All these people—young babies, pregnant mothers—

how can they be dangerous? The whole thing is so outlandish that you can't believe it.

Tanforan was awful. My brother and I didn't have proper clothing or equipment—just had a whisk broom to sweep out all the manure and dust in our stable. The smell! We cleaned the stall, stole lumber, and turned our stall into a home. Adapt and adjust right away, that's my whole nature.

You could hear all the people crying, the people grinding their teeth; you could hear everything. Even lovemaking. It turned out that the barrack that my brother and I were in was a special stable for young married couples. Later on this neighbor came quietly to me and said we ought to move because we weren't married. I said, "If there's any moving to be done, it's going to be you because we're all settled." But everything ended well. We were never home.

Miné Okubo, Plate II, nine photostat negatives from *Citizen 13660.*

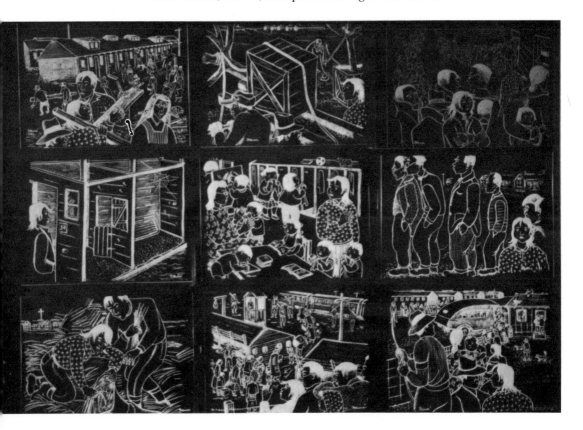

I was always busy. In the daytime I went around sketching. There wasn't any photographing allowed so I decided to record everything. Observing. I went around doing all these minute sketches of people and events. I didn't sleep much.

I worked all night at the newspaper. It was lunacy to work all night, going twenty-four hours a day. I was art editor for the daily newspaper and art editor for *Trek* literary magazine.

I made many friends in camp. Those working on the newspaper and many others. With ten thousand people in a mile-square area, everybody knew everybody. There were many interesting people. I was considered quite a character. There was absolutely no privacy, so I nailed up a quarantine sign to discourage visitors. I would say I had hoof and mouth disease. I still have the sign. You have to live the camp life to know what it was like.

Miné Okubo, Arrival at Camp (Topaz), gouache.

When visitors came, they had to stand in the middle of the highway. And all the cars would go by and they would yell, "You Jap lovers!" So I discouraged my friends from coming.

In Topaz the barracks were better—clean except for the alkali powder dust. We stole right away all the lumber and things. Those that came late didn't have anything. We went out at night, falling into ditches and pipes. It was just chaos. Deep ditches with humps of dirt because they were still building the camp. It was dark as the ace of spades with no lights anywhere. It was quite an experience.

They had hobby shows in camp, very well received. Everybody in camp displayed their talents. They made use of everything in camp. Rocks, pebbles, fruit wrapping, seeds, cardboard, fence, anything they could find. Clever, beautiful, interesting. I did a huge collage using rolls of toilet paper. They didn't know what to make of it. Gave many a good laugh though!

70

I taught art in camp to children. I liked the children and students. It is a two-way learning—we learn from each other. Each one is an individual and needs individual attention. It was interesting. I remember the girls drew pictures about camp and camp life. The boys were more imaginative. Their pictures were on war, airplanes, circus, and subjects out of camp.

But for the children, camp wasn't too bad. Children can take anything. Everything was a circus to them. But it was hard on the old people and mothers with children. Children attracted children and they would run off to play.

In camp I kept myself busy. I knew what I wanted to do. All my friends on the outside were sending me extra food and crazy gifts to cheer me up. Once I got a box with a whole bunch of worms even. So I decided I would do something for them. I started a series of drawings telling them the story of my camp life. At the time I wasn't thinking of a book; I was thinking of an exhibition, but these drawings later became my book *Citizen 13660*. So I just kept a record of everything, objective and humorous, without saying much so they could see it all. Humor is the only thing that mellows life, shows life as the circus it is.

After being uprooted, everything seemed ridiculous, insane, and stupid. There we were in an unfinished camp, with snow and cold. The evacuees helped sheetrock the walls for warmth and built the barbed wire fence to fence themselves in. We had to sing "God Bless America" many times with a flag. Guards all around with shot guns, you're not going to walk out. I mean . . . what could you do? So many crazy things happened in the camp. So the joke and humor I saw in the camp was not in a joyful sense, but ridiculous and insane. It was dealing with people and situations. The humor was always, "It is fate. It can't be helped. What's going to happen next?" I tried to make the best of it, just adapt and adjust.

Like growing up in Riverside, California. We were poor, so I got used to living by my wits. My oldest brother, like Robin Hood, attracted all the rebellious and lost. They were good people, very idealistic, but off the main road. Children, young people, adults gathered in our backyard every day: at night fifty, sixty people around a bonfire telling stories—ghost stories, crime stories, fairy tales. There were all kinds of sports and games—boxing and wrestling. It was great fun. I was just a shy little girl watching. Very shy, but very observing and wanting to know everything. If anybody talked to me, I would run to the next block!

In our family my mother and father were real disappointed because all the children were independent-minded. We listened but we would not follow. None of us would go to Japanese school, so we talked mixed-up Japanese and English. They were disappointed to think that everyone's children

were becoming doctors and dentists and all of their children were complete monkeys, I mean real birds on the creative side. Well, of course, Mama and Papa were both creative too. She was a good artist and a calligrapher, and he was a scholar. But Mama encouraged me from the beginning. I used to follow her around with paints and brushes. . . . That's my beginning.

I'm coming from parents who suffered so much and were so persecuted. I had already seen life. I always observed. Even at that time, I saw how you are basically an individual and different, and society is trying to make you the same, so it can control you. So, being off the main road, I decided I'm always going to have some trouble.

I am not bitter. Evacuation had been a great experience for me because I

Miné Okubo, Evacuee Children, charcoal.

love people and my interest is people. It gave me the chance to study human beings from cradle to grave, when they were all reduced to one status. And I could study what happens to people. At the beginning they were all together—comradeship and humor—but as camp grew, they started becoming status conscious, bettering their homes, being better than Mr. Jones. Just like what happens in the establishment. People are people; everywhere it's the same. Only the backdrop and stage is different. Just have to change the scenery. People have the same concerns for home, family, comfort, security, and loads of problems. That's all there is when you come to think of it.

So how people reacted to the evacuation depends. There are different personal reactions to everything. Disaster always brings change both good and bad. Certain people get bitter, vengeful. I am a creative, aware person. Like I said before, an observer and reporter. I am recording what happens, so others can see and so this may not happen to others.

73

I was planning on staying in camp; I didn't have any money and at least I was being fed! Then I got a telegram from *Fortune* magazine. I had always thought that if you are patient enough, the gods would answer your prayers. So I left for New York. I had my belongings in great big crates sent to *Fortune* magazine, since I had no other address. They had no idea what to do with all my things. There was no room in their ancient little cubby-hole office. During the war it was next to impossible to find a place to live in New York, but they all went out looking for places for me.

One woman from the magazine saw my camp ink and rice paper sketches and suggested I write a book. It was so difficult getting it published. At that time anything Japanese was still rat poison. Columbia University Press saw the value of my story and printed it in 1946. Gradually, interest developed and my drawings were exhibited all over the United States. But it was really too soon after the war. Anything Japanese was a touchy subject.

So I went into commercial art and did everything from soup to nuts. But it took me ten years to realize that commercial art was just an establishment game, not what I wanted. I'm an individual who wants to contribute to the betterment of this world. To me, life and art are one and the same. It took me forty years to find this out, but now I have arrived. The key is simplifying. I deal with the highest value of vision: what reality is and what it is not. I only simplify the content of reality into my own imaginative writing. By mastering drawing, color and craft, I express the content of reality—that which is universal and timeless. It's a long, lonely road, but there's no other way. In my next life, maybe I'll come back as a Japanese beetle!

7

History II: Camp Life

Life inside America's concentration camps was just that—everyday life with all its joys, sorrows, achievements, disappointments, complications, and tensions, but all behind barbed wire. That paradox, normal living under abnormal conditions, characterized all aspects of camp life. To its credit, the WRA attempted to transform the artificial communities into less alienating ones. But when a family apartment proved to be nothing more than a bare room in a barrack, food was army rations served communally and in scant portions, wages for mandatory jobs were set at nineteen dollars and under per month, and armed guards watched the internees' every move, failure was assured. If the inherent tensions seldom erupted in violent outbursts or massive organized protest, they were there nonetheless.

On arrival at the assembly centers, evacuees were given a series of shots, assigned an "apartment," reunited with the few pieces of permitted baggage, handed a mattress bag, pointed toward a mountain of straw, and instructed to stuff themselves mattresses. Many of the apartments were former horse stalls; paint had been slopped over the straw and the dirt-covered walls. They were smelly; the manure stench was unbearable in the hot summer months. And they were loud; every sneeze and scuffle echoed through the building. Privacy was nonexistent, as were comfort and convenience. The inconvenience was small, however, compared to the actual health threat each person faced. At Santa Anita, for example, hospital records showed that 75 percent of all reported illnesses could be traced to life in the horse stables.

But with the move to relocation centers and the realization that they would be there more or less permanently, the incarcerated Japanese Americans resourcefully conquered their environment. When they realized the only furniture provided would be army cots, the residents built tables, chairs, and shelves with materials from the camps' scrap lumber piles. They hung sheets and blankets as makeshift walls in their undivided rooms.

The unpartitioned communal latrines outraged many and were a source of grief until the camps closed. For all, however, the mess hall situation was probably the worst. At first, the food was terrible, the diet poor, the portions inadequate, the lines insufferably long, the wait boring, and the insult of having to take food from the government too hard to bear. As days became months, chefs became more experienced and the rations improved slightly. Meals in the centers, nonetheless, remained a miserable experience.

Work projects were started as well. Evacuees staffed the mess halls, maintained the facilities, ran the schools, organized clubs, wrote the newspaper —in essence, did everything to keep the community in working order except govern and supervise. These privileged functions were performed by the Caucasian staff. Defense work was begun in several of the camps, most notably a camouflage factory in Santa Anita. The administration hoped such projects would give the internees some sense of control over and respect for the environment, discouraging rebellions. In addition, it was a way for the interned people to contribute to their upkeep.

Although the relocation centers to which the internees were transported after a few months were brand new and supposedly permanent, their physical conditions only replicated those in the assembly centers. WRA Director Eisenhower testified before a Senate appropriations committee at the time that the construction "is so cheap, that frankly if it stands up for the duration we are going to be lucky." Chief Justice William Denman of the Ninth Circuit Court of Appeals noted in an opinion of August 26, 1949, that conditions in no federal penitentiary were so poor. Five to eight people shared one 20-by-25-foot room. Two hundred fifty to three hundred shared the same mess hall, laundry room, latrine, and recreation hall. As in the assembly centers, food was very bad. As time passed, the discomfort of the living situation only became aggravated by the intense boredom of concentration camp life.

To dispel that boredom, the WRA initiated a social welfare program, which stipulated that all able-bodied residents who wanted to work be provided with jobs and vocational training. Jobs were in mess operations, construction and sanitation, project administration, agriculture and land development, internal security and fire protection, and consumer enterprises. For a standard work week of forty-four hours, the majority of laborers were paid sixteen dollars monthly. According to the WRA program guide, "apprentices and those who require close supervision" earned twelve dollars per month, and professionals and "those with difficult duties or supervisory skills" took home nineteen dollars per month. This salary scale was insulting to the evacuees and proved controversial. The army had previously stated that wages would be eighty dollars monthly, but that was quickly amended to no more than twenty-one dollars monthly, the prevailing pay for a G.I. On top of room, board, and wages, the WRA provided a monthly clothing allowance of three dollars and fifty cents for each adult, three dollars for each dependent aged between eight and fifteen, and two dollars for each dependent under eight. At the six centers where the climate was more severe, the monthly allotment was twenty-five cents higher.

To further its claim that the camps were American "pioneer communities," the WRA set up in each camp a government (Community Council) of and for the evacuees. At the same time, however, it qualified that government's power to the point of nullifying it. The Nisei-dominated Community Council, composed of one representative from each block of fourteen barracks, was perceived by the older, more experienced Issei for what it was— "a baby's plaything." Its duties included advising the WRA camp director and ensuring that rules and regulations were enforced. The camp director maintained absolute power of veto. The WRA also encouraged the residents to publish a newspaper that would serve the community. Yet these papers were severely restricted. "Like all other newspapers in the U.S., relocation center papers will enjoy full freedom of editorial expression. The Project Director, however, may suspend publication of the newspaper at any time if this seems necessary in the interest of public peace and community security," the WRA program guide stated. Such constraints underscored the contradiction of living behind barbed wire in a democratic country.

These pioneer communities were rife with tension, and the WRA's social welfare policies only exacerbated the generational and cultural divisions. Conditions might have deteriorated further had it not been for many concerned and sympathetic Americans who withstood the insulting epithet "Jap lover." Many Quakers and other pacifists came to live alongside the Japanese in the camps, working as teachers and administrators. They helped to place qualified Japanese Americans in jobs outside and found them sponsors and homes, facilitating the relocation program.

From its inception, the War Relocation Authority's policy was to move Japanese Americans out of the western defense zones and into midwestern and eastern communities. The WRA launched the "seasonal leave program" in late July 1942, at the pleading of intermountain farmers, to save the sugar beet crops of Utah, Idaho, Montana, and Wyoming. Laborers had to be citizens who had never lived or studied in Japan. These Nisei, nearly 10,000 at work by October 1942, returned to the camps following their work periods. The prejudice and harassment some of these laborers met dampened others' desire to leave the camps. At the same time, the National Japanese American Student Relocation Council, under the auspices of the American Friends and others, persuaded reluctant West and East Coast educators to open academic doors to deserving Nisei. Some 4,300 students left the camps for college under this program.

Other Nisei left to join the armed forces. In mid-1942, the Selective Service had assigned a draft classification of 4-C to the Nisei and Kibei, placing them in the ignominious category of enemy aliens; many young, enthusiastic Nisei perceived that rating as another slur on their loyalty. Six months later, however, the Secretary of War announced formation of a special segregated combat team of Japanese Americans and called for volunteers, 1,500 from Hawaii and 3,500 from the mainland. These volunteers were to become the famous 100th Infantry Battalion and the 442nd Regimental Combat Team —the American units with the highest casualty rates and most decorations of the war. The War Department stated as its rationale for creating the segregated fighting units that the performance of a separate unit of Nisei would be noticed and could serve as conclusive refutation of charges of disloyalty. The announcement was followed by intensive propaganda within the camps. Volunteering was advertised as the "golden opportunity" to "secure" one's future as an American. More than 1,200 Nisei volunteered for combat and about two thirds were eventually accepted for military service. That figure fell far short, however, of the War Department's quota. The refusal of many Nisei to volunteer could be interpreted as protest against their incarceration.

A policy permitting "indefinite leaves" began in the fall of 1942, extending relocation privileges to anyone who could pass a stringent security clearance. The WRA set up field offices in major U.S. cities and relied on benevolent organizations and individuals to help the Japanese Americans reenter mainstream society. As preconditions of relocation, the WRA required confirmation of employment and recommendations from Caucasian friends. Japanese Americans had to report subsequent changes of address and remain under scrutiny tantamount to parole—extraordinary conditions applied to free citizens. The program required officials first to ascertain the sentiment of resettlement communities. If it was unfavorable to their presence, Americans of Japanese ancestry were not permitted to enter. That paternalistic stipulation had its roots in the unfortunately very real racism, sometimes violent, which many had faced early on. The WRA's "indefinite leave" policy, therefore, had to be accompanied by a WRA promotional campaign not only to mitigate evacuees' fears of what might happen to them outside the camps, but also to reeducate a paranoid public to differentiate between the enemy across the Pacific and fellow U.S. citizens.

78

A significant part of the evacuated population, nonetheless, remained in the internment camps until their 1945 closing. Throughout their stay, evacuees' attempts at improving conditions and policies within camp most often met with resistance or disregard from the administration. After the return of the community's leaders from Department of Justice detention camps in late 1942, Issei groups were able to initiate more resolute demands for changes. Workers organized, calling for everything from more milk for children to improved living conditions and better pay. Interned Japanese nationals could make their complaints known to the Japanese government through the Spanish Consul, who responded by conducting inspection tours of all the concentration camps. Harold L. Ickes, secretary of the interior, wrote to Roosevelt in April 1943 about the increasingly explosive situation: "Information that has come to me from several sources is to the effect that the situation in at least some of the Japanese internment camps is bad and is becoming worse rapidly. Native-born Japanese who first accepted with philosophical understanding the decision of their government to round up and take far inland all of the Japanese along the Pacific Coast, regardless of their degree of loyalty, have pretty generally been disappointed with the treatment that they have been accorded. Even the minimal plans that had been formulated and announced with respect to them have been disregarded in large measure, or at least, have not been carried out. The result has been the gradual turning of thousands of well-meaning and loyal Japanese into angry prisoners. . . . [This] bodes no good for the future."[1]

Confused WRA policies were primarily responsible for this potentially volatile situation. Each camp experienced strikes and work stoppages, and in Manzanar and Tule Lake, martial law was briefly declared to stem violent demonstrations. In Manzanar, some of the most extreme pro-Japan, anti-WRA Issei and Kibei (the initial evacuees from Terminal Island, near Los Angeles, and hence most victimized and embittered by the evacuation) were forced to live alongside some of the most active and patriotic members of the JACL. In December 1942, violence erupted over an allegation of pilfering food. Militant Issei and Kibei harassed Nisei JACLers and called them *inu* (dogs; that is, informers for the FBI). The situation got out of hand. The administration spirited "intended victims" to the safety of the military garrison; troops armed with submachine guns and rifles moved into the camp. The angry crowd surged toward the jail where an immensely popular Kibei leader was being held. The army threw tear gas and fired, instantly killing one internee and mortally wounding another. Martial law was imposed for two weeks. Fifteen "trouble makers" were arrested and removed to heavily guarded isolation camps. After the Manzanar revolt, there were protests, demonstrations, and strikes in all the camps over the many inequities, but other serious violence was avoided until the crisis at Tule Lake in late 1943 and early 1944 resulting from the loyalty questionnaire and the subsequent segregation policy.

The issue that sparked the most contention was the so-called loyalty questionnaire instituted by the WRA in early 1943. Initially the WRA used a Selective Service document entitled "Statement of U.S. Citizens of Japanese Ancestry, Selective Service Form 304A." All draft-age Nisei men were required to answer its more than eighty questions, in particular numbers 27 and 28. Although the fact was nowhere stated during the "registration" process, as it was called by the government, answers of yes to both marked the evacuee as "loyal" and an answer of no to either characterized him as "disloyal." Question 27 read: "Are you willing to serve in the armed forces of the United States on combat duty wherever ordered?" Question 28 asked: "Will you swear unqualified allegiance to the United States of America and faithfully defend the United States from any or all attacks by foreign or domestic forces, and forswear any form of allegiance or obedience to the Japanese emperor, to any other foreign government, power, or organization?" The WRA thought the questionnaire would be useful in their relocation program and adapted it for Issei of both sexes and all female Nisei seventeen or older as well. They retitled it "Application for Leave Clearance" and modified questions 27 and 28. Addressed to female Nisei, the former now read: "If the opportunity presents itself and you are found qualified, would you be willing to volunteer for the Army Nurse Corps or the WAAC?" For both female Nisei and all Issei, question 28 now ran, "Will you swear unqualified allegiance to the United States of America and forswear any form of allegiance or obedience to the Japanese emperor, or any other foreign government, power, or organization?" The latter question was rewritten again after it caused much confusion among the Issei ("Will you swear to abide by the laws of the United States and to take no action which would in any way interfere with the war effort of the United States?"), but only because of expressed dissent. The questionnaire was initially administered as if it were mandatory. Only in February 1943, after they encountered resistance, did the WRA rule that it was not compulsory.

Because the "loyalty screening" was supposed to facilitate relocation, no administrator had expected opposition to the questionnaire, but registration was anything but smooth. There were acts of civil disobedience among the hitherto extremely law-abiding people, including noncompliance, and mass requests for repatriation and expatriation. The questionnaire caused irrevocable distrust of the government's policies and its spokesmen, the WRA and FBI. And it devastated families, many of whom were split over how to answer the infamous questions 27 and 28. The seemingly simple procedure proved to be arduous and divisive. Compliance differed from camp to camp depending on the relationship between internees and administrators. Of the nearly 78,000 inmates eligible to register, almost 75,000 eventually filled out the questionnaire. Some 6,700 answered no to question 28; 2,000 qualified their answers, so they too were considered disloyal by the government; a few hundred left that question blank. About 65,000 answered yes to question 28. At five camps everyone registered, and at four others a total of thirty-six—ten aliens and twenty-six citizens—refused. But at Tule Lake, 3,208, almost a third of the camp population refused to answer the questionnaire, and the process which had been expected to finish in ten days took two months. The reaction resulted from hostility between internees and the inept administration at Tule Lake—which, knowing that the registration was not compulsory, nonetheless decided to arrest all those who refused to participate. These arrests totaled 140 and foreshadowed trouble to come.

Registration "failed" at Tule Lake, and to a lesser degree elsewhere, for a number of reasons, miscommunication being the most important. Nobody knew what the questionnaire was for. Both its titles and the poorly worded questions caused much confusion. "Registration" implied it was compulsory; "Selective Service Form" seemed to mean that an answer of "yes, yes" was as good as volunteering for the army; "Application for Leave Clearance" was interpreted by many Issei worried about what might happen to them on the outside as implying that two yes answers would force them to leave the safety of the camp. Issei, particularly in Manzanar, reacted negatively to question 28, with its phrase about forswearing allegiance to the Japanese less persons. How could they declare unqualified allegiance to a country that denied them the opportunity to become citizens? Many Nisei read question 28, with its phrase about foreswearing allegiance to the Japanese emperor, as self-incriminating, much along the lines of "When did you stop beating your wife?" Not wanting to fight against brothers and cousins in Japan, many Nisei saw the registration process as the restoration of only one of their confiscated citizenship rights—the right to be shot at.

The unexpectedly mixed results of registration (aggravated by a so-called fact-finding tour of six camps by segregation proponent Senator A. B. "Happy" Chandler of Kentucky, and exaggerated newspaper reports of the Tule Lake noncompliance situation) were the impetus behind Senate Resolution 166 of July 6, 1943. Strongly supported by War Department officials, the JACL, and nervous relocation center directors, the resolution called for a physical removal from the camps of all "disloyals"—all those denied leave clearance on the basis of their questionnaire answers, all who refused or failed to respond to the registration call, and all who asked to be repatriated or expatriated. Such people were ordered once again to move, this time to a new "maximum security" Tule Lake relocation center. "Loyals" originally interned at Tule Lake were moved to other relocation camps.

The result of cramming 18,000 people—some militantly pro-Japan, but most merely confused—into a space meant for 15,000 was tragic. Given the camp's incompetent administrators, who were also in some cases bigoted, and the trigger-happy military police guards, the potential for violence loomed. The underlying discord among internees and between internees and administration exploded in late October–early November 1943. After a truck accident in which one evacuee died, internees organized a work stoppage to protest widespread administrative neglect, incompetence, and corruption. A visit by WRA Director Dillon Myer on November 1 prompted another massive protest over these unanswered charges. As internee protests continued, California and national newspapers increasingly magnified their importance. When the army entered the camp (on November 4) and instituted martial law (on November 13) the media reported that the "Jap Rebellion" in Tule Lake had been suppressed. Curfews and military searches and seizures became the rule, and a stockade was erected within the camp where "leaders" of the insurrection were imprisoned. About 400 people were detained in this stockade for periods ranging from one to nine months without being charged with any crime. Hunger strikes ensued to protest the inhumane conditions in the stockade. But it remained intact and in use until August 1944, when it was razed, only after the American Civil Liberties Union threatened to file habeas corpus suits on behalf of two of its many inmates.

Mismanagement in Tule Lake acted only to polarize already embittered and confused people. Within the Tule Lake camp a strong minority movement for what was called "resegregation" grew up. Its proponents were staunchly pro-Japan and objected to the presence of a majority who, despite their presumably "disloyal" status, had no such orientation. In preparation for their eventual expatriation, these resegregationists conducted Japanese cultural activities. They easily won recruits among the frustrated, idle, impressionable young Tule Lake internees.

New government actions only compounded the tragic misunderstandings. On July 1, 1944, Congress passed Public Law 405, the so-called denaturalization bill. A compromise measure, it was an alternative to a number of more punitive and constitutionally dubious bills calling for a sweeping deportation to Japan of Americans of Japanese parentage. The law provided that an American, with the attorney general's approval, could renounce his or her citizenship on American soil in time of war. The de facto rescission of the West Coast exclusion orders in December 1944 effected a quick closing of the relocation camps. Instead of being seen as the long-awaited release from unfair bondage, however, since it came at a time when war with Japan was still raging, it was perceived by the Tule Lake "disloyals" as a cruel and capricious move—"another double cross." They would have to resettle in the United States now, the country that spurned and hated them. After the attorney general approved on December 23, 1944, the renunciation applications of 117 Kibei, the Justice Department was flooded with 2,000 applications. From January 11 to March 17, 1945, a Justice Department team held renunciation hearings in Tule Lake. At the final count, 5,461 Americans—seven of ten Tule Lake Nisei—signed away their citizenship. The other nine camps had a total of 128 renunciants, further evidence of the culpability of Tule Lake's administrators.

The repatriation and expatriation, indeed all the violent excesses at Tule Lake, were just one extreme, albeit a revealing one, that resulted from the WRA's policies. There was another extreme as well—the experience of people for whom the evacuation was nothing but positive. But for most internees, life behind barbed wire was a constant and moderate pain, tolerable only when they did not dwell on it. The contentious issues—insufferable living conditions, unrewarding work, intense boredom—compounded or diminished by administrative action, were present in all the camps. And the most divisive issue of all, the one that split father and son, husband and wife, was the question: "If we are loyal, why are we behind barbed wire?"

8

The Sour and the Sweet

Hiro Mizushima

They called it a relocation camp, but it was a concentration camp. There was barbed wire. They told us the machine guns were to protect us, but the machine guns were pointing toward us.

When we first went into the Stockton assembly center, we didn't know what to do. Everything's uncertain, you know. Everything was very confusing. People were wondering "what the hell are we? Are we American or are we foreigners?" And finally we got this classification of 4-C—enemy alien!

When we were in the assembly center we had a notice that we were going to Arkansas. I was getting disgusted with the assembly center anyway, just being cooped in. In the beginning it was a novelty, but afterwards, this kind of life wasn't what I wanted. If I was going to the army, or to war, fine. But not being cooped in an assembly center as an enemy alien. That was awfully frustrating.

When they came recruiting for army volunteers, they said we had to prove ourselves. I felt why should we prove ourselves? The government has to prove itself to us first. And we had these loyalty questionnaires in camp. That was a very mixed emotional thing. What could we say? In order to leave the relocation center, your answer had to be positive. There were a lot of emotions that you had to confront.

But we were too damn young to be thinking too seriously. Asking which girl to go to the next dance might have been just as important as going into the army.

Jack Matsuoka

This business about proving our loyalty—when they first asked us those

84

Gene Sogioka, Volunteering for the Army (Poston), watercolor.

questions, I thought: My God! I didn't know how to answer. It just struck me as stupid. Why should I have to answer that? We saluted the flag every morning, and to ask us that. . . . Some government official called me and some other guys in and wanted to know why we weren't enlisting in the army. And it just ticked us off that we would be asked such a question right in the camp. I guess we gave him sarcastic answers, and he just shouted at us: "Are you citizens or not?" That question itself was so stupid. They just scared us; I thought we were going to end up in jail.

Atsushi Kikuchi

I remember the loyalty questionnaires, but they didn't seem to bother me . . . I think I had more faith in the United States than a lot of people. Just had to bear it out; it's going to be over someday—that was more or less my attitude.

85

Jack Matsuoka, "I Pledge Allegiance . . . " (Poston), pencil.

George Akimoto

I had a couple of arguments with my old man about Japan declaring war in that fashion. And I told him, "You know, eventually Japan is going to lose, I don't care what you say. A little country like that, tackling somebody this big, you're not going to win. Eventually, you're going to lose. It's a matter of time." And he didn't believe me, although it turned out to be true.

My father, after they sent him back from Bismarck and Santa Fe [Justice Department detention camps], was so angry. He was going to take all of us, send us to Tule Lake, and from there to the exchange ship back to Japan. I refused to go. I told my old man, if you want to go, you go ahead, but I'm not going to go back. This is my country here. And finally he changed his mind and decided to stay.

Charles Mikami

A lot of people wanted to go back to Japan, and I told them, "Don't go back. Japan has hard times now—America bomb; everything flat." You got

86

to use your head. "Don't go back. You'll want to come back to America again." But at that time, you can't come back.

People would say, "Japan's better, Japan win," like that, you know.

I say, "No, I don't think so."

They say, "You're terrible; you're pro-American."

"No, I'm not pro-American. Japan now has big battleships and strong army, but Japan has no oil, no rubber. Maybe keep up for a while, but they can't go on. So I don't think so."

But "Mr. Mikami's pro-American," they say.

So I got to keep my mouth shut. I don't say anything. Just painting, no meetings. I'm instructor of art, that's enough. So I had a nice time in the camp—quiet.

Ron Wakabayashi (1983)

There was a lot of courage in all parts—whether you said "No, no" or volunteered for the 442nd, there's courage on both sides.[1]

Lawrence Sasano

Everything was done on a regimented basis, more or less, because you have so many groups from diverse occupations, different areas, and different attitudes. To put all these groups together and try to make a more or less harmonious environment is difficult to imagine. So there was always friction, one way or another: second generation against second generation; those who didn't, shall we say, care one way or another and those who did—pro and con—about being thrown into camp. It would be typical of any human being. It wasn't unusual because we were put behind those barracades. So I won't say that being confined in camp brought about disagreements or disappointments or this sort of thing. I think that is typical of life itself. As I say, you have to take the sour with the sweet. I think that sums it all up. If there was confusion, disagreement, misunderstanding, arguments in camp, I think we cannot say that's typical of camp life. I think this is typical of what we experience anywhere else—in a camp or in a big city.

Wrinkles

Three long years of camp life
have increased as well
the wrinkles.

Forty years of uphill struggles

and only the wrinkles
    on the face to show for it!

The cream of the crop—
    Nisei soldiers—
        by wrinkles on the parents brow.

On close scrutiny
    my wife is also
        at that age of wrinkles!

Tears welled up
    at the sight
        of father on parole
        [from a Justice Department detention camp]

The forlornness of his wrinkles
    emphasized by his decision
        to be a permanent resident.

—Anonymous[2]

Frank Kadowaki

We were worried. We didn't know what our lives would be. See, we didn't know the next day—that we worried about. We're all together in one camp; so many camps in the United States scattered all over. In Poston, 15,000 in one camp. Surrounded among the barbed wire, see. We cannot get out. And all guards standing everyplace. And we don't know what our life going to be. I mean, are they going to kill us or . . . ? We didn't know what the next day might be.

We had a terrible time. Like my youngest son, when he was in camp, he was seven years old. When we went in they gave us typhoid shots. But I think they made a mistake or something because after the shot, next day, he became crippled—still crippled; he's using a cane right now.

Lili Sasaki

We didn't know what to expect in the camps. We didn't know if we were going to stay there forever, or if we were going to be sent back to Japan. Or if something got real bad, and Japan was winning, they might kill us all. If Japan did start to win, I think the camps could have been invaded. Some of the hot-headed ones would have said, "Blow them up." That was a frightful thing. It could have happened because there was prejudice.

88

Harry Yoshizumi, Poston, watercolor.

I was very rare. . . . I was different. I deliberately went into camp to see what it was like. Something told me this is going to be something so wild and different. And I don't regret going into camp. I'm glad I went in to see what kind of thing was happening, although I am against exactly what happened. It's just that I wanted to go in to see what it's like. I never lived among Japanese, really. Our family lived in small towns. I couldn't imagine what it was like to wake up in the morning and see nothing but Japanese. And now I know.

Life in camp was strange in a way. It's like a small Japanese town. They all live close together. And when you walked away you could hear them talking. The old timers when they got together would read out loud. And sometimes when I passed a house I could hear the oldsters, some grandfathers, reading a newspaper just like a play. And then I could hear some Nisei say, "Oh, Grandpa, don't read like that. People can hear you." They're ashamed.

89

Matsusaburo Hibi, Topaz in Winter, woodcut.

Anonymous Journal Entry, Poston (1943)

Mrs. C. T. said last night that when the small children play around the block, often they say, "Let's play killing the Japs." The older people look at each other sadly, but they don't say anything because they think the children are too young to explain to them. They don't realize "Jap" and "Japanese" mean the same thing.[3]

Haruko Obata

Some of the young children were confused about the recent turn of events. I remember one six-year-old saying, "I don't like Japan. I want to go home to America." He thought that if all he saw were Japanese faces he must be in Japan.

My Mom, Pop, and Me

My Mom, Pop, & me
Us living three
Dreaded the day
When we rode away,
Away to the land
With lots of sand
My mom, pop, & me.

The day of evacuation

Unidentified, Self-Portrait (Topaz), postercolor.

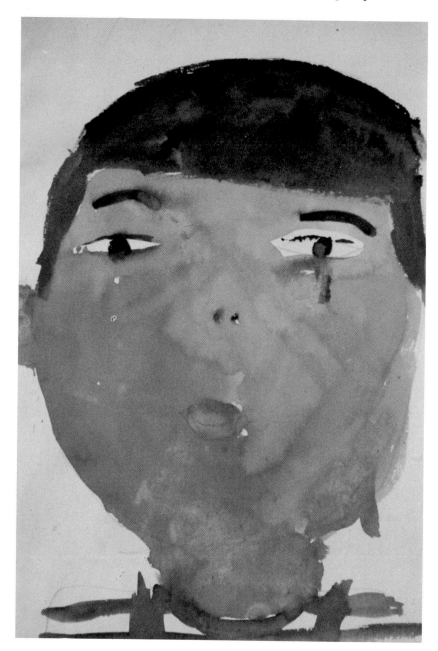

Unidentified, Self-Portrait (Topaz), postercolor.

We left our little station
Leaving our friends
And my tree that bends
Away to the land
With lots of sand
My mom, pop, & me.
—Itsuko Taniguchi[4]

Jack Matsuoka

When the school first opened, they didn't have teachers, no books. So just go to class to hear somebody talk, that's about it. I had my heart set on going to college, but once I got in the camp I gave up studying totally.

It's so hot and so crowded, we all went outside to sleep. We'd talk, just talk all night long—about girls, sports, boys, the army. Next day, you had a hard time getting up. So for us kids, just get up, eat, and play, that's all. Every now and then have a dance party. So it wasn't that bad for us.

Yuri Kodani

For the kids it was great. We didn't have to get home for dinner because there were mess halls all over and we could just stop in with our friends.

To our Fellow-Americans,
Deep from out this lonely desert's vastness
We, the Japanese-American youth,
Innocent of wrong,
Firm in our Hope and our Faith,
Cherishing forever the ideals of our Native Land,
Striving to build in the wilderness,
Struggling to build our Destiny,
Extend to you
our
Fellowship.
—Poston Junior Red Cross
Club Scrapbook Preface[5]

Hiro Mizushima

A typical day in camp had its pluses and minuses. We got up about 7:30 or 8 o'clock. I was able to take a shower whenever I wanted to—this was one of the pluses—so I took a shower whenever I had the chance. Then breakfast in the mess hall; we shared the same food. Then we were picked up by truck to go to the office. I was teaching elementary art in the assembly center for a

94

while. I thought teaching wasn't just for me. Somebody happened to ask me to work for the [news]paper. I had no idea of what commercial art was; I was taking up fine arts. I said I'd try anyway. We did the illustrations, doing the heading for the paper, things like that. At Rohwer, I was co-art editor of the paper, *The Rohwer Outpost.* The newspaper hoped to just tell the story of what's going on in the camp. There were mixed emotions because the staff had to satisfy the people who were interned and also those who were in charge of the camp.

So we went to work and worked on what we had to, it's not real hard work, but we're only getting [nineteen dollars] per month, so we didn't have any incentive. That's one of the things that bothered us: we lost our incentive to do things, to accomplish things. But at least this paper kept me going. Doing something, anyway.

I just couldn't get down to the idea of painting or drawing in my free time.

Ibuki Hibi, Watchtower, Topaz, pencil and watercolor.

The thing was, there wasn't that much free time. You know, on the paper you would be working day and night at times to meet that schedule. When you had time, everybody else is playing baseball or doing something else. On top of that, art materials were quite scarce at that time. And like I said, you weren't in any mood to paint.

George Akimoto
Outside of the confinement, it was a normal life, except we all ate in the mess hall. [Lil Dan'l, the cartoon character Akimoto invented] tried to see the humorous side of things. And it wasn't all that tragic. We weren't exactly

Unidentified, Tanforan Grandstand, crayon.

at Buchenwald. Only thing that was so bad was that our future was so indefinite. We didn't know what was going to happen to us. But once the relocation started, people started leaving camp, and then it got a little more hopeful. A lot of the guys volunteered to go in the army. I remember a couple of guys were the first to volunteer to get out of camp, to go in the army. And they were across the river, right across the Mississippi at Camp Shelby, so they would come back on weekend passes once in a while. But gradually more and more guys volunteered to go into the army. Some of them went overseas and got killed.

[Food was all right] most of the time. In the assembly center we were on C-Ration, I think, or K-Ration. But one of the things I remember is that every-

George Akimoto, Impressions of Rohwer in camp newspaper *The Rohwer Outpost*.

body was complaining about the effects of the army rations on their sex lives, because the cans were loaded with saltpeter, I guess to control the sex urges of personnel in the army overseas. And this is the stuff they were feeding us!

George Akimoto, Impressions of Rohwer in camp newspaper *The Rohwer Outpost*.

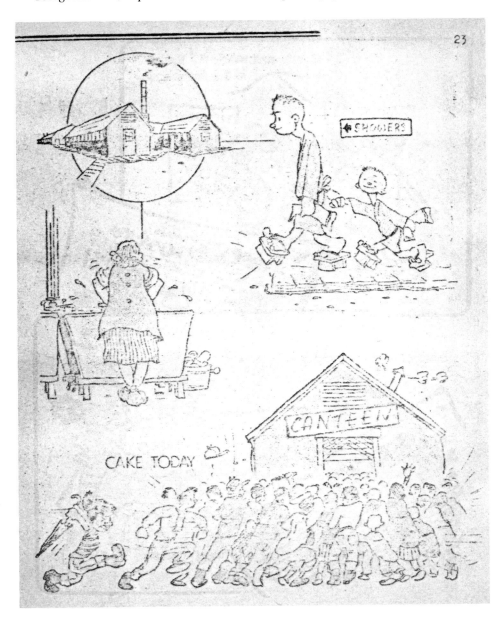

A lot of things are not mentioned in any of the histories of evacuation. One thing that stays in my mind was when we were in the assembly center, we had some real bad people running the camp—not running the camp, but employees within the camp. One night we got wind of—they're shipping big sides of beef into the camp to feed us, yet we were getting nothing but canned stuff, rations. And once we heard rumors they were smuggling the sides of beef out of camp and somebody was selling them black market. So we sneaked over and watched one night, and sure enough they were loading this truck full of sides of beef. And we heard there was an FBI spy in camp, so we made sure he found out about it; yet nothing was done. I suppose we could have printed something in the paper, but, you know, that would have caused a riot in the camp.

Then there's an instance where some guy in charge of our mess hall ordered this special kind of rice—not the kind that's usually fed to people, but there's a special kind of rice he ordered through channels. And the shipment came in, only whoever brought the order in didn't know it was the kind of rice that you make sake from! So these guys were brewing sake in the camp. Made their own stills and they're brewing sake in camp from the rice that was specially ordered through the government.

The first thing they did was give everybody shots. They were giving, I guess they were army overseas shots—three shots that they usually give in three different days—bang, all at once! So people were walking out of the clinic and just fainting from the shot.

Another thing when we were in Arkansas, the MPs who were put in charge were all complete misfits, guys you couldn't use in combat. So there were guys that weighed three hundred pounds and guys that were so skinny they could hardly walk, and cripples—guys like that guarding us in camp. And when we first went in there, they had watch towers up with machine guns. And one night, one of the guards decided—he was drunk I guess—he sprayed the roof tops with this machine gun. And after that, they removed the machine guns. But, you know, you don't read about things like that.

I think you could catch just about every type of snake in the United States there in Arkansas. So we started a snake collection. We were walking down the road one day with a six-foot timber rattler. This old lady came up, wanted to know what it was. When she saw what it was, oh, she screamed! And she had a laundry basket. She threw it up in the air and just took off down the road!

Life in camp really wasn't that bad, especially in Arkansas. Once we got there, the camp started its own farm, growing vegetables. Everybody had a victory garden right by their barracks. And then they had a pork farm also. And everybody had their own jobs—some people were paid sixteen dollars a month and others were paid nineteen dollars a month—which was kind of silly. But Sears, Roebuck did a tremendous business! Yes, everybody had a Sears catalogue and ordered things.

100

Frank Kadowaki

The government supported us with food, and I was teaching artwork, so I get nineteen dollars a month. I taught oil painting and watercolors. But we had a terrible time getting supplies. We can't go out of the barbed wire, you know, and we were asking the camp people to get supplies from the outside. But we can't get what we want.

I worked on a Japanese garden for the administration. They gave us a truck and permission to go out and pick up the rocks. We'd drive out fifty to seventy-five miles away from camp to bring back rocks—oh, we feel paradise!

Charles Mikami

I had lots of time in camp to paint. Government gave us food, you know. When I paint someplace inside camp, a lot of people come to see. They say, "Mr. Mikami, how much you going to sell this for?" I can't sell here, or rumor go around: Mr. Mikami is selling lots of pictures and making lots of money. That is no good. So I can't get money.

"Well, I'll tell you," I told them, "you got a hobby, maybe making stone sculptures, we exchange." I told them, "See, you got a hobby, and I got a hobby." So I have two trunks in the basement of things! I can't charge money, because I get nineteen dollars and that is enough for spending because the government gives me food and clothing, everything. So, no argument.

In Pinedale there is no time to paint. But at Tule Lake, I had to get job anyway. That's the rule. Government says you have to do something. "I think I clean up toilet or something like that and get sixteen dollars," I said.

"That's full now, so you do something else."

"All right, I'll teach Japanese brush painting."

"That's fine."

"All right. But I have no brush, no paper."

"Oh, paper and brushes, administration give you; everything they give you."

So block manager told everybody, "Charles Mikami is instructor of Japanese brush painting, so if you want to learn, report. . . ." Right away, about thirty came.

Instructor got permit to go out of barbed wire. So I took my class outside of barbed wire. When you go out, you have to report how many are going out. At most thirty people. I take water and color or dark sumi. The guard says, "All right." Sometimes I give him a picture, so he doesn't ask me. "Oh, go on," he says, "You are all right. You are harmless." So we have a nice time.

Suiko Mikami, Snowstorm at Topaz (1944), watercolor.

Masao Mori

Camp life wasn't too different—except I had time for sketching. Otherwise there, I work. Nineteen dollars a month! I was chief cook for Block 30; I lived in Block 29. I didn't know anything about cooking, but I thought to myself that the only thing people enjoy is dinner or dinnertime because there's nothing else to enjoy in camp. So I try to do the best I can. Nobody taught me. Some ladies knew how to cook, but they just helped serving. They used to sing, a lot of people inside the mess hall, "Mori-san, I like the way you cook!"

I cooked whatever they brought me. So the food was not so bad. Once they brought me a big piece of meat, taller than myself. But I had to decide how I am going to cut this for 350 people. Oh, it was hard. Sugar was limited because of the war.

102

When I was cooking there, I cooked for 350 people. Oh, I was busy. We had two shifts, morning and evening. But then they changed it; one worked all day for two weeks. Then you were off and another group takes care of the cooking. So that's why I had plenty of time to do drawing. Oh, I enjoy drawing so much. I go outside the camp sketching. First three or four months we can't go out, but after a year or so, we can go out all right. I did a lot of sketching outside the camp; I have some sketchings inside.

For the first time the Isseis had time: they weren't slaving in the fields. They made all these beautiful things. We had a whole barrack full of exhibits, clear to the ceiling. You should see the things that were made—everything you could imagine: carved things, sewing, embroidery. Even people that didn't know what to do, they found little rocks and they wore out pants, they said, polishing, making little things. For the first time they became creative, because they had time. Which proved time is the essence for everybody. If you don't have time, you have no time to be yourself. You'll just be two dates on a tombstone.

We decided that since we were being fed, we might as well go into art, since we have the time to. I made quite a few figurines, all given away to friends. Some of them broke. I only have one left. I got local clay from Colorado. You could not fire it in a kiln, you had to do it in one of these stoves, so naturally it broke. It's made out of that local red soil.

They gave us all jobs. We all had to work. You know the wages they paid us. I got sixteen dollars! I was teaching junior high school, teaching adult school—arts and crafts or something for the older folks at night. They provided all the art supplies. Not much, but children's color crayons and paper and glue, colored paper. That's about all you had. So you had to make lampshades out of paper, batik. They did things like that. Any clay you could get around the place, you'd make things from. Carving or polishing stone, carving wood and roots that you could find around there.

And of course, Japanese love clubs. We were clubbed to death in all the camps: sewing clubs and poetry clubs and this and that. Right away, we put together a writers' club, artists' club. Even an exercise club. I could get up in the morning, and I could hear them exercising. The Japanese are organizers, right away they are organizing.

We also put on plays. We decided we might have dancing—got all the musicians who could play jazz or records. So we did have a lot of dances. We decided that we are going to have dances and let the people have fun.

George Akimoto

Half of the camp was from Stockton/Lodi area. The other half was from parts of L.A. So you know a bunch of country bumpkins like us were mixed in with some of the zoot suit crowd from L.A. I remember when I first went into camp they had these dances. Half the group would be dancing all over the floor, the other half would be standing in one spot, with their zoot suits and gray pants, dancing pachook style. And within a month or two, the southern Californians were dancing like the northerners, and the northern Californians were dancing like the southerners.

104

Yonekichi Hosoi, Mess Hall (Topaz), watercolor.

Gene Sogioka, Recreation Barrack Dance (Poston), watercolor.

The only thing hard for the Nisei, younger people, was that they were losing two, three years of the most important part of their lives, when they should have been out getting an education or getting established in business. That's what we lost, outside of our pride.

The old folks, they didn't know whether they were going to end up dying in camp or what. They had more to worry about. The ladies would get together and play cards, mah jong or whatever. They had poetry classes and that sort of thing. Every block had a recreation hall, and some of the older folks would get together and work on their crafts. I remember hearing the old folks worrying about what's going to happen to us if we end up here the

Hisako Hibi, A Day in February (Topaz 1945), oil.

rest of our lives. "Are we going to end up like the Indians, you know, selling carved birds and weavings for a living?"

Jack Matsuoka

Sports were real important. We'd get up and play basketball, baseball. I was on the basketball team and I helped coach football. I remember we had to buy our own baseball and basketballs from Sears, and our own uniforms and set up our own league. We had championship playoffs. It's funny, but I think sports were one of the key factors that kept people from going astray, or feeling dissatisfied in camp. If it weren't for those athletic leagues, I think there would have been more dissension.

Manzanar

Dust storms.
Sweat days.
Yellow people,
Exiles.
I am the mountain that kisses the sky in the dawning.
I watched the day when these, your people, came into your heart.
    Tired.
    Bewildered.
    Embittered.

I saw you accept them compassion, impassive but visible.
Life of a thousand teemed within your bosom.
Silently you received and bore them.
    Daily you fed them from your breast,
    Nightly you soothed them to forgetful slumber,
Guardian and keeper of the unwanted.

They say your people are wanton
    Sabateurs.
    Haters of white men.
    Spies.
Yet I have seen them go forth to die for their only country,
Help with the defense of their homeland,
America.

I have seen them look with beautiful eyes at nature.
And know the pathos of their tearful laughter,
Choked with enveloping mists of the dust storms,
Pant with the heat of sweat-days; still laughing.
    Exiles.

And I say to these you harbor and those on the exterior,
"Scoff if you must, but the dawn is approaching,
When these, who have learned and suffered in silent courage;
Better, wiser, for the unforgettable interlude of detention,
Shall trod on free sod again,
Side by side peacefully with those who sneered at the
    Dust Storms.

108

Siberius Saito, Line at Canteen (Tanforan 1942), pencil.

Sweat days.
Yellow people,
Exiles.

—Michiko Mizumoto[6]

Atsushi Kikuchi

There was a long line when you wanted to go to mess halls. People who had jobs had special passes to go through, so we didn't have much of a long line. But some of the people who had to go through the regular line, especially in the beginning, collapsed in the street waiting under the hot sun.

Hisako Hibi, Mothers Bathing Children in Laundry Room (Topaz 1943), oil.

Hisako Hibi

My camp scenes were mostly painted on the canvas as I saw them—objects seen. I did not paint purposely, nor consciously, but the paintings speak for themselves. They tell the social conditions at that time.

Lili Sasaki

Most of the people were making idealistic paintings—Japanese looking like this and holding their hands up to the clouds, or little child there showing that we were looking for hope, that kind of thing. But they weren't mak-

Lili Yuri Sasaki, My Santa Anita Barrack Room, watercolor.

ing it very realistic. I wanted something to show exactly what kind of camp we were in. So that's why I painted that one. So I'd remember.

I tried to make my room look pretty. Everybody did that. The walls were just bare wood. I knew that we were going to leave and that we were going to be sent to another camp. I thought I wanted to have something to remember exactly what my room was like and what I had in there. That's why I painted that [picture]. I decided I'm not going to make it like others' [paintings]. And that's exactly the way it was—white wood, cots put together, bed spread, so I painted everything. From the little bed there, you could take four little steps and then there were steps to go down and you were out. So that's exactly what it looked like, and I'm glad I did it. Just the same coloring, and every knothole that was in there.

111

Yoshiko Uchida, Tanforan from the Grandstand, watercolor.

Sometimes they'd knock the knotholes out and peek into the next room. Yeah, boys would do that, when they had the young girls in the next room. They'd laugh about it and put the knothole back. And the young kids did hate to live with their parents in such close quarters. No place to go, except to the grandstand with their girlfriend or something. In the evening we'd often take a walk around the racetrack for exercise.

Shoes all wore out because of the fine gravel. Pretty soon we wanted shoes badly. They hadn't organized yet so we couldn't order them. So we started making wooden shoes—getas. They made them quite well. They'd get boards, and old tire rubber, and they put it on the bottom so it doesn't make too much noise and wear out. So I had one made too. I got so that I liked them.

It was a conflict because the Isseis and the Niseis, they're both living close together. Before camp we only went around with the Niseis; we didn't have much to do with the first generation. They were our enemies in a way. Now,

112

Eddie Sato, Making Wooden Shoes, pencil.

MAKING WOODEN SHOES

that's a funny thing to say, but we didn't like them when we were teenagers. And yet we had to get to know them, had to get along because we were living in the same barrack with just a little paper in between. My neighbor wanted to paint, but he couldn't make the color turquoise, so I helped him, and he helped me. I got to know him, and I thought, well, he's not so bad. These oldsters—we used to call them oldsters—they're human, they're nice.

One very interesting thing, a couple of artists (Caucasian teachers) and their wives decided to live in with us, in our block. You see, all the Caucasians lived way in the corner of the camp. But they said, "Since we're working, teaching here, we'd like to live with you." They got into a lot of trouble with the administration. They told them to stop: "You must come back because you put us in a bad. . . ." But they wouldn't do it.

So it wasn't long before the superintendent of the school and his wife

113

Hisako Hibi, A Letter from Her Son in U.S. Army (Topaz 1945), oil.

said, "We're going to live among the Japanese." And they also came in our block. Yes, so they were the only ones who decided to live with the Japanese, within our barracks instead of in the corner area. And they ate in our dining rooms. And then another couple came, so three couples total.

Finally they weren't too strict, and they said, "All right, so long as there is room." So they came and stayed. And every night we'd go and visit them. And then when we had dances we invited everyone, and certain people always came to our dances.

114

Gene Sogioka, Train to Poston, watercolor.

You know what we got hungry for more than anything else? Food. We got so tired of the camp food. And it got so we couldn't stand looking at the women's magazines with all the jellos and cakes. We wanted to go home and bake a cake or something. Oh yes, we just got so tired of camp food. They just handed you a tin plate all mixed up in one. And we missed the Japanese tea. We got orange pekoe type. Did you know toward the end, we all got accustomed to that? When we got out, Japanese tea tasted bitter.

Finally, they said if you're cleared maybe you could get out of camp and go to Lamar. That was the closest town. Granada just had a saloon. But fifteen miles away is a town—Lamar—big enough to have a Woolworths-type store. And I looked forward to going there. So I wrote a letter and went to

115

the postal department in camp and I said I would like to go the next time the postal truck goes in. I got my clearance and I got to go. And my goodness, it was the biggest thrill to go to a store. I bought hair pins and little tiny yards of different colored ribbon for my daughter, and friends told me to get this or that—erasers, funny little things. It was such a big treat to get out there.

When I was in camp, my brother died. My youngest brother was killed in an auto accident in Nebraska. I got the news when I was in camp, and I couldn't believe it. I kept saying, "It couldn't be true; I hope it's not true." I was crying the whole night. And yet the teenagers next door, beyond the thin wall, kept playing "Don't Sit under the Apple Tree" and all this dance music when I wasn't in the mood to hear it. But I remember crying all night long with that kind of music going on. So loud. Whenever I hear that, I think of me crying all night long thinking "I hope that it's not true, I hope it isn't true." They had to have the funeral in camp. My brother brought the ashes and he had to give it to my mother over the fence.

When I was leaving camp to relocate to Cincinnati, I had to leave at the crack of dawn. It was still dark, I remember. Yet my friends all got up and made a special breakfast for me. They took me to a tiny, little station in Granada. I was the only one there with my daughter. And it was dark, and all the barracks in the field were silhouetted. They wished me good luck.

9

Kango Takamura

I was photo retoucher at RKO Studios until Second World War, when I went to camp. Every morning after Pearl Harbor, I tried to go to studio and always stopped. Afraid of what's ahead, you see. I'm afraid. Everyday, not safe. Even in the studio.

During wartime, though, people at RKO Studios were so kind to me. They helped me; everyone of them helped me. "Come on Tak, I watch for you," [they would say].

One time, right in front of RKO Studios, one actor [says], "Your people!" —points like this at me—"Pearl Harbor!" He looks terrible, you see.

My boss [reprimanded] him so he won't say anything after that. And then [my boss] said, "Hey Tak, this is trouble. You have to watch out. This kind of fellow is all over around there, so you have to watch out." Every day they were so nice. Some people understand so much, sympathize for us.

And in the wartime, we don't get any jobs, I think. I hated the fact that I was born in Japan at that time, but only at that time. The Japanese third generation talk lots about it now. They say we were Americans so not supposed to [be interned]. But for us, it's very protective, see.

When he told us over the phone he was eighty-eight years old, not feeling well, and spoke very poor English, but would love to talk with us, we did not know what to expect from our visit with Kango Takamura. The frail but energetic, softspoken man who met us at the door to his house in December 1982 ushered us right in as if we were old friends. He seemed decades younger than his real age. As he regularly hopped up to answer the telephone or his wife's questions, or to run and get a painting or article to show us, we found ourselves increasingly captivated by our host.

After apologizing profusely for his poor English (which was not half as bad as he claimed), and explaining he had had a stroke a while ago that had affected his speech, the kindly man, without any prompting from us, began reciting his story:

The FBI had a list of leaders. Some people who were on it were very young. They are feeling very bad, especially the young people just educated in Japan. They come back from Japan to this country because Japan and China were fighting, and supposing they had stayed there, they would have had to go fight in China. Now they are under the American flag, so they talk. Young people talk against the American flag. That's showing off, you see. Inside, they feel different; they talk, that's show off. I was not talking like that. But I was on their list too.

Once there was a famous captain in Japan who came here to this country just before Pearl Harbor. He was very proud, and he don't know anything about America. I think you can judge what kind of character he was — during the Japan-China war he killed a hundred Chinese soldiers. One day, he said, he didn't know anything that was happening behind him, but unconsciously he pulled his sword like this, just a movement, and the Chinese soldier was coming at the same time. He killed the soldier. Just unconsciously he did like this. Terrible. He is very good with the sword. That's why he is proud, very proud. I invite him to our home and have dinner together. He's talking about that kind of stuff. Unfortunately, the FBI outside was watching him.

And another thing, he wanted to buy a movie camera. We had three movie cameras at RKO Studios. And one camera was cheap, very cheap, because RKO wanted to sell that camera and wanted to buy another new one, you see. So this man, the captain, was very happy to buy that one. "Soon as you get the money, please send that camera, all right?" he said. We promised that, and he went back to Japan. But as soon as he went back to Japan and telegraphed to me, that order was canceled. At that time, no orders could come anymore from Japan to this country. That's why canceled. So it's all right. It's nothing for me. But FBI knows everything.

So I was on the list from FBI. They came about two months after Pearl Harbor. I have nothing wrong; I never against this country, so I'm all right, I thought. But their point is different. You are either for America or for Japan. Pro-America or pro-Japan.

"For what did you want to sell to Japanese army that camera?" one day they ask me.

"Oh, I want to make money!" I said. I thought I'd get several hundred dollars' commission. But, of course, I don't think about that. . . . So anyhow, I was arrested, went to wartime prison.

118

Kango Takamura, Our Guard in the Watchtower Became a Spring Baseball Fan at Santa Fe, watercolor.

OUR GUARD IN THE WATCHTOWER BECAME A SPRING BASEBALL FAN AT SANTA FE.

First night I was very afraid. I think I am the only one in the United States arrested. I was arrested and made to sign all kinds of things and photographed. And taken to the jail. Meanwhile, inside the jail was a very famous head of Japanese ship company. He thought he was the only one being arrested, and I thought I'm the only one arrested. Oh, he was very, very happy because he found out he was not the only one. We went to the jail at the City Hall. Oh, I was very nervous, because it's wartime, you know. Then after about one week there, we were transferred to a war camp. And then transferred to Santa Fe, New Mexico.

As you know, we cannot use any camera. So I thought sketching's all right. But I was afraid I was not supposed to sketch. Maybe government

Kango Takamura, After the Baseball Games at Santa Fe, watercolor.

doesn't like that I sketch. . . . So I work in a very funny way purposely, made these funny pictures.

Very often we play baseball. This is the kitchen band. And always the umpire said "fifty-fifty"—nobody wins or loses. Always fifty-fifty. And after that, they made noodles for people, you see. So people appreciate so much. This is the way we play. And sometimes the ball runs over the fence and then the guard would come down and get it. He liked it so much.

Also when I was working at Santa Fe, I painted a picture every day on the mess hall door. Every day I painted celebrations or once in a while I painted very funny pictures. Everyone liked those pictures. I was so busy every day, so busy. Nobody stopped me. That's why I got a little bit better. Little by little, I sketch more like a photograph.

One day we saw a wonderful cloud to the South. It was evening time. Oh, it was a big cloud. All pink. I had never seen this kind of cloud before. Really

Kango Takamura, Lucky Cloud (Santa Fe), watercolor.

Kango Takamura, First Impression of Manzanar (June 1942), watercolor.

FIRST IMPRESSION OF MANZANAR.

JUNE 1942

I was surprised. So we called it a "lucky cloud." "Look at the cloud. It won't be long, this war," we said. So everybody was very happy. We say it is a "Lucky cloud"—sign that war is over. This is atomic test, I think. But it was a little bit early then, so many people think that's odd. But I don't know. Still I don't know.

Everyday I was working for the office making signs. It was very convenient for the administration, so they wanted to keep me there. I had been there about three or four months. And little by little the men had been let out from there. Everybody thought I'm one of the first ones that will be allowed to get out. But my name was not called. So one day people called Washington, D.C., and they said, "Ah, Takamura is already gone. Takamura went to Manzanar," they answered. "How come Takamura is still there?" Already long time I had been able to go free. But the office answered, "He's very use-

Kango Takamura, Progress after One Year, the Mess Hall Line (May 19, 1943), watercolor.

PROGRESS AFTER ONE YEAR. THE MESS HALL LINE

ful, so we keep." I was supposed to leave after three months, but I stayed there a little over four months or maybe five months.

And finally I was released and went to Manzanar. We arrived at Manzanar in the early morning, before sunrise. Beautiful. All pink. The mountains around there were all pink. So beautiful. Yes, I thought this is such a nice place. I joined my wife, and daughter, and her husband, and granddaughter and stayed there three years. I worked so hard there. Every day I enjoy. Usually when I worked in the movie studios I would work eight hours. But every day at the camp, I worked ten hours. I was happy. I moved into a barrack in the very corner, Camp 35. Nobody was there. Just snakes, such a wild place! Only the lumber was laid down, that's all. So we had to tarpaper and put waterlines in. And little by little. . . .

This was my first impression of Manzanar. Oh, it's really so hot, you see, and the wind blows. There's no shade at all. It's miserable, really. But one

Kango Takamura, Manzanar High School Commencement (July 3, 1943), watercolor.

APPROXIMATELY 200 STUDENTS GRADUATED AT SECOND MANZANAR HIGH SCHOOL COMMENCEMENT. July-3-1943

year after, it's quite a change. A year after they built the camp and put water there, the green grows up. And mentally everyone is better. That's one year after.

We had a visual education museum. We go outside the barbed wire with special permission. Every day we go collecting Indian stuff and all kinds of stuff around there to build the museum for children's education. Fortunately, we had a head with lots of experience. He was working for the Chicago museum; he knows about museums. But after he went East to teach Japanese, they wanted me to be the head.

So I said, "I'm just a poor artist. That's all. I have no experience at all, no idea at all. What should I do?"

And the principal said, "If you don't want to do it, we will close this mu-

seum. So will you or not? It is no matter how poor your English is. That doesn't mean anything to me. Do as I say."

So I said, "All right. Thank you." Then I start. I work so hard after that. Every month we had an exhibition—flower exhibition or art exhibition. Every month. So every day I have to work hard after that. Where I live in Camp 35 to the museum is nearly one mile. It's a long way. Sometimes, you know, I walk three miles—this end to the other end of camp and again like this, up and down, like this.

You are not allowed to shoot photographs. That's why I sketch exactly what was, everything I saw. It was exactly like this.

This is the first graduation. The people were very proud; we built the school ourselves. Very proud. And every one of the teachers is highly educated. They were American Hakujin (Caucasians), American teachers who tried to understand Japanese. It's wartime, but they sympathized with people who live in this country. They know such people are very obedient, every one of them. We don't make trouble, they understand. And the students at that time were especially good, I think. Very quiet, nice students really. Many times I teach the kids how to sketch. Very often I did, and I enjoyed it so much. I taught lower classes, children about ten years old, eight years old.

This was a very happy day for me—pounding "mochi" [a Japanese rice delicacy]. We have to have mochi on New Year's Day. Every family does. So this was a very happy day. People did not expect us to get mochi, you see. Maybe even in Japan you had to be very fortunate to get mochi during the war. We are in an "enemy" place, yet we have mochi. We appreciate so much. That's what I sketch.

Really our life was not so miserable. Everyone was writing songs and learning how to paint and studying and writing poems. It is not so miserable a life. After the war is over, people thought it was a miserable place. But it was better than Island people in Japan had, I think, because we at least had plenty of food. Of course, not such good food! Funny thing is that it was not such good food, but very few got sick because of the food. You see, it's not gourmet stuff, but good enough for health. And plenty of water. Japanese people make big baths with cement, and we got in there together, not individually, but five people, seven people, ten people all together. So very nice.

In those days, you know, we don't think about wartime. Sometime we forget. It was so peaceful up there. It was very peaceful because the younger people who made too much noise and trouble, they went to another camp [Tule Lake].

My nature doesn't like trouble. I am afraid, you see. I don't want to see any blood. [During the revolt] about fifty people came to my daughter's place to get her husband [Togo Tanaka, who had been identified with the JACL]. I was among them because I want to watch my daughter and grandchild. I'm afraid they try to hurt my daughter. The army came after that to protect them, and I took my grandchild to the army car and she cried. So afraid, you see. I said, "Don't you cry, Jeannie!" I scold like this, and she stopped crying. She understood—only one year old. She stopped right away. "Please take this baby to her family over there," I said. And they took her and moved them to the army camp that night. So we are safe. Every day I was so afraid. My daughter was with us, and her first child, a little girl who was born just after Pearl Harbor, almost one year old.

One morning I couldn't open the door. I push and push, but I can't open

Kango Takamura, Winter Snowstorm (Manzanar, February 22, 1944), watercolor.

the door. I thought maybe people had nailed down the door. I thought that because some people thought my family was too much pro-America. I was afraid, you see. But I push and push and the snow comes down. That's what I sketched.

After that, we were so quiet. Every day was good. We had success making rubber. In Salinas, ten years before the war, they had started, but they did not have success making rubber. But one day accidentally we made wonderful rubber. We sent it to Salinas. Oh, they are surprised! They have never seen such good rubber. So right away, an engineer came to us and asked, "How did you make this rubber?" But the farmers did not keep exact records. So it took them a long time to make the same kind of rubber again. Fortunately we had a teacher from Cal Tech, Dr. Emerson. He loved us so much that during the war while gasoline was being rationed, he rode his bicycle everyday to save gasoline, so he could drive to Manzanar and guide us

127

Kango Takamura, Students Hurry to Classes . . . (Manzanar 1943), watercolor.

STUDENTS HURRY TO   THE CLASSES   BELLING'S ON THIS FOGY MORNING K. TAKAMURA FEB — 1943

on how to grow rubber. So I sketch the guayule flower, the leaves, everything, by using a magnifying glass. And Dr. Emerson took those pictures to Washington, D.C. Right away they gave us fifty thousand dollars to study rubber growing. In those days, fifty thousand dollars was really big money. So really, we had a nice time up there.

So many Eastern studios want me [to leave camp and work for them], but I don't want to go there. I want to go back to RKO Studios in Hollywood.

[Before living in California I had lived in New York.] From Japan I came to Hawaii and stayed there about ten years. Then I came to New York. I got a job at New York Paramount Studios. That's the main office, on Long Island. Gloria Swanson was there, and director D. W. Griffith. I wanted to become assistant camera man. That's why I came to this country. But someone told me, "You are too short, too small." Back in Japan as a child I had wanted to be an artist. But in Hawaii, I saw an exhibit of all kinds of [modern] paintings. But I don't understand these. This is not a place to learn art, I thought,

128

I think photography is very beautiful art, you see. That's why I became photographer and not artist. At that time in Hawaii I was earning almost three dollars and a half. But even at that time, that's not enough to live on. So in the evening at the motion picture theater, I play. They give me fifty cents each night. It helps lots. It's a funny life.

Unfortunately at that time, every day I had a headache. I couldn't go to school, so doctor sent me to church; I attend school evening time. Ten years, my head is empty, no education at all. But I have such a nice memory of those ten years in Hawaii. I like children so much, see, so at that time I studied about fairy tales and wrote fairy tales and lived with children. Every month we told fairy tale stories at Sunday School, we taught Japanese fairy tales. Club members were all over Hawaiian islands. Each school was a member. So every month we did a fairy tale at each school.

Anyway after I came to New York, funny thing was I didn't get headaches at all that summertime. Every day I had had a headache, but that summer, no headache at all. Why? I think. I had my glasses changed. Before that I had glasses, but they didn't fit. I couldn't see right. My whole story, I think, may be different.

I came back to RKO Studios after the war and the people were really surprised to see me. I'm retoucher, you see, and the president usually never says, "Good morning" or something like that. But when I came back to the office, the manager and the president came to my place and welcomed me back. Twenty-five years I continued to work over there, until 1957 when they closed the studio.

But anyhow I am eighty-eight years old already. I enjoy this country so much. A nice life, I had. I like this country so much, you see. Just to visit Japan is all right, but I cannot stay there. I cannot. My character is not a fighting spirit, no. In Japan [it's very competitive]. I am eighty-eight years old, but I think if I were in Japan, long time ago I would have died.

10

History III: War Hysteria

Anti-Asian discrimination on the West Coast preceded the arrival of the Japanese. One of its goals was an end to all Asian immigration. When significant numbers of Japanese began to immigrate in the 1890s, forty years after the Chinese, specifically anti-Japanese agitation also made its appearance. Its chief proponents were economic protectionist groups such as the Native Sons of the Golden West and the xenophobic newspapers of William Randolph Hearst. In addition, state-sanctioned discrimination — the ineligibility to be naturalized or to own land, for example — relegated the Japanese to second-class status. But the immigrants were determined to overcome these obstacles. The Japanese had uncanny success in agriculture, cultivating land previously deemed unarable with enviable productivity. Their percentage of the dollar volume of California's crops usually far exceeded the percentage of its agricultural land that they worked. It is no wonder vehement attacks on them came from protectionist groups.

As relations between the United States and Japan became increasingly complex and tumultuous in the 1930s, the voices of intolerance, of economic protectionism, and of race hatred were amplified. The Oriental Exclusion League (a coalition of anti-Japanese groups) and the West Coast media continually harped on the "Yellow Invasion" from the Far East. Not only were the Japanese racially inferior to Caucasians, the exclusionists maintained, but they retained an undying fealty to the emperor; never could they become true Americans. Pearl Harbor was used as a convenient pretext for intensified lobbying on the part of these nativist individuals and groups for the removal of all Japanese from American society.

Starting in December 1941, and continuing through the next three months, newspapers reported supposed incidents of Japanese subversion and sometimes called for vigilante acts against members of the guilty race. Sensationalist stories announcing sightings of enemy planes and ships and possible poisoning of food and water supplies aggravated the already tense situation. With the Japanese rapidly advancing in the South Pacific at America's expense, what began as an understandable, though unfounded, fear of a coastal invasion gained the paranoid dimension of fifth column activity on the part of enemy alien residents. Once the Roberts Commission, set up by Roosevelt to investigate the attack on Pearl Harbor, alleged subversion perpetrated by Japanese Americans in Hawaii (a claim later found to be false), the call for mass evacuation began to attract serious discussion.

That there was war hysteria is beyond question; the country was stunned by the attack on Pearl Harbor. But without the professional anti-Japanese agitators who preyed on the nation's debilitated spirit, a mass evacuation might never have surfaced as a viable plan. In refusing to recognize individual distinctions among the members of the Japanese race, the anti-Asian press and pressure groups punished an entire community. General DeWitt most concisely voiced the prevailing West Coast sentiment when he addressed the House Naval Affairs subcommittee on April 13, 1943: "It makes no difference whether the Japanese is theoretically a citizen. He is still a Japanese. Giving him a scrap of paper won't change him. A Jap's a Jap."[1] And some of the most influential and well-respected liberals could be heard propounding similar arguments. On February 12, 1942, journalist Walter Lippmann wrote: "Since the outbreak of the war there has been no important sabotage on the Pacific Coast. From what we know about Hawaii and the Fifth Column in Europe, this is not, as some have liked to think, a sign that there is nothing to be feared. It is a sign that the blow is well-organized and that it is held back until it can be struck with maximum effect."[2] Earl Warren, one of the United States's staunchest defenders of civil liberties (then attorney general of California), was one of the evacuation's loudest proponents. One of the few to oppose the evacuation was Norman Thomas, who called it "a good deal like burning down Chicago to get rid of gangsters,"[3] and went on to note: "What is perhaps as ominous as the evacuation of the Japanese is the general acceptance of this procedure by those who are proud to call themselves liberal." Swept away by war hysteria, liberal New Dealers found themselves in a curious consensus with reactionary good ol' boys who had been clamoring for the removal of the Japanese for years.

As early as October 1941, the United States had broken Tokyo's code and learned that Japan was contemplating an attack, the probable target Hawaii. Roosevelt assigned Special Investigator Curtis B. Munson to ascertain the loyalty of residents of Japanese descent, both Hawaiians and continentals, in the event of such an attack. Munson worked with the full cooperation of naval and army intelligence and the FBI. In November he submitted a detailed report to the president, who then circulated it among all high-ranking cabinet members, including Secretary of War Henry Stimson. The report stated, "The story was all the same. There is no Japanese problem on the coast. There will be no armed uprising of Japanese."[4] Munson's findings seemed to deny the military necessity for any mass evacuation of America's Japanese. But his report was to be ignored.

Immediately after the attack on Pearl Harbor the president issued Proclamation 2525, which enabled the FBI to interrogate and detain all those who were thought to be Axis sympathizers or otherwise suspicious. During the next several days more than five thousand Issei and Nisei men were questioned and arrested. Leadership in Japanese social and church groups was interpreted as questionable activity; searches for contraband—radios, cameras, and Japanese literature—in "enemy alien" homes were commonplace. But although the FBI's criteria for suspicion might seem capricious and harsh, only what amounted to little more than 1 percent of the West Coast Japanese population was eventually detained on its orders, compared to the 100 percent later incarcerated by the military/civil authorities. The FBI worked quickly and thoroughly to allay the public panic caused by the attack on Pearl Harbor.

In Hawaii, where one might have expected the greatest panic, the issue of how to deal with the Japanese community was managed fairly by General Delos Emmons, the U.S. Army commander there. Thirty-two percent of Hawaii's population was of Japanese descent. The sheer numbers made mass evacuation an impossibility without jeopardizing the economy and hence the war effort. Like the FBI, moreover, the Hawaiian military command found it could maintain control over the resident Japanese community by arresting suspicious individuals. Not one act of subversion occurred and the rights of individuals were preserved, even under martial law.

Despite these ample assurances that the Nikkei posed no military threat, the frenzy of war carried along the plans for a mass evacuation of the West Coast. Naval intelligence reported in June 1942 that the Japanese fleet was so seriously damaged at the Battle of Midway that there was no threat of a West Coast invasion. Yet Colonel Karl Bendetson responded that because of continuing military necessity the evacuation must proceed as scheduled. At that time, 90,000 American Japanese had already been interned, and by early August almost 110,000 had been forcibly removed and incarcerated. Clearly considerations other than national security figured in the escalated evacuation proceedings.

General DeWitt, who had been put in charge of the Western Defense Command, was a career army administrator determined to prevent a Pearl Harbor from happening under his charge. Not very highly thought of by his peers, DeWitt was essentially a confused leader whose advisers—California-born and raised Colonel Bendetson, chief of the alien division of the army, and General Allen Guillion, provost marshal—were widely perceived as prejudiced against the Japanese. They had begun campaigning for evacuation as early as December 19, 1941. Both were skilled lawyers; with one ear to public opinion and one eye on career advancement, they persuaded an originally reluctant DeWitt of the military necessity of the evacuation. Between January and February they met with a succession of officials in the Department of War and the Justice Department in an effort to get the go-ahead for their plans. High-ranking military officers such as Chief of Staff George C. Marshall dismissed their idea outright while U.S. Attorney General Francis Biddle said the Department of Justice could not condone such drastic excesses, especially as applying to citizens. Biddle added, however, he would not oppose the conduct of a mass evacuation by a civil agency, so long as it was under military auspices.

Bendetson's and Guillion's constant lobbying, coupled with increasing public pressure for action, eroded the high command's initial resolve. On February 11, 1942, Secretary of War Henry Stimson spoke with Roosevelt, whose authority was needed to abridge the rights of approximately 70,000 citizens on the grounds of military necessity. Assistant Secretary of War John McCloy reported to Bendetson the result of the meeting: "The President in substance says go ahead and do anything you think necessary . . . but as he puts it, 'Be as reasonable as you can.'"[5] To enable the army to circumvent the Department of Justice (in effect, what Attorney General Biddle had suggested) and hence the Constitution, Bendetson developed a plan. He would have an executive order issued which would authorize the secretary of war to designate military areas from which people (specifically, though unstatedly, Japanese) could be excluded by virtue of military necessity. Although Biddle and some of the more level-headed members of the government made last-minute attempts to forestall the evacuation, by that time it was too late. Only J. Edgar Hoover opposed it, for such a move usurped the FBI's authority. Behind the shibboleth of "military necessity" the removal of Japanese and Japanese Americans was virtually uncontested.

The president had ultimate authority. He signed the evacuation order. One can only conjecture why. Clearly, he was preoccupied with war responsibilities, and he probably did not consider the liberty of 110,000 people to be a high priority when the country was at war on two fronts. But Roosevelt was a politician; 1942 was an election year and the evacuation could be seen as a tactical move: Domestically, the order mollified the West Coast. Internationally, the incarcerated Japanese might be used as pawns in affairs with Japan. No one, Roosevelt and the Supreme Court included, questioned the military necessity. In the name of expediency, Roosevelt signed Executive Order 9066, allowing the Western Defense commander to begin the exclusion.

DeWitt issued public proclamations ordering the mass evacuation, and Congress passed Public Law 77-503 fixing penalties (fines of up to $5,000 plus imprisonment) for violation of his military restrictions. On March 27, DeWitt halted the free movement of Japanese from the West Coast and initiated a regimented military one. He also announced that while awaiting their evacuation, all Japanese in Military Zone 1 were subject to a curfew between 8 P.M. and 6 A.M. and restricted to traveling not more than five miles from their homes without special permission.

Evacuation notices posted on street corners ordered the head of each family to go to one of the sixty-four local civil control stations for family tags—numbers that would identify their baggage and themselves. They were told they could bring one duffel bag and two suitcases each. In these, they must have bedding, linen, clothing, and eating utensils. All private and sentimental possessions had to be discarded or stored. The Farm Security Administration was to see that the Japanese got a fair deal on their crops and real estate; the Federal Reserve Bank was to safeguard the evacuees' other property. But inept, insincere, and insensitive management coupled with fear and general skepticism prevented the evacuees from getting the help they needed from these agencies. The government did little actually to assuage the staggering loss of real, personal, and intangible property. Businesses, homes, cars, appliances, were sold under immense time pressure; the profiteers were ruthless, offering ten dollars for a brand new refrigerator and the like. Only altruistic groups such as the American Society of Friends, church organizations, and trustworthy friends stood as buffers between the Japanese community and the opportunists. The monetary loss is astounding. Approximately $73 million of prime farm land in Military Zone 1 alone was left, deeded over, or sold at a pittance, with crops yet unharvested.

Since most of the community's leaders—Issei males—had been spirited away by the FBI and placed in Department of Justice internment camps, the Nisei, mostly teenagers, were left in charge. Few had any political acumen or experience; the community had no spokesmen. So when the government forced them from their homes, they obeyed. With a long tradition of respecting authority and a recent history of expecting discrimination, they could do little else. The evacuation order met with some overt challenges, but for the most part the community complied. To prove their loyalty, they would be better Americans than Americans and give up their civil rights. The confused legacy of Pearl Harbor—the shock of war with Japan—left the Nikkei even more dumbfounded than it left the rest of America.

11

You Can't Black Out the Stars

Hiro Mizushima

December 7, 1941, was Sunday. I was going to the California College of Arts and Crafts and we had an assignment to do some drawings of Lake Merritt in Oakland. I went there early in the morning and about 12 o'clock, I was ready to return home. A couple of sailors came up to me and said, "Are you Chinese or Jap?" I said, "I'm an American. Why?" They just glared at me and walked away. I got onto the streetcar to return home and I hear all these sirens. I heard this announcement for all military personnel to report to their bases. I thought all this was awfully funny. When I finally returned home, I still didn't know what was going on. I turned on the radio and I heard about Pearl Harbor. I didn't know where Pearl Harbor was or anything.

My father's hair turned white the day of Pearl Harbor, I think because he didn't know what the future would hold, and he had one brother in the old country. First thing my dad was saying was "well, if something happens, I'll be the first one to go into camp or something." But at that time, we didn't even know about the camps.

Atsushi Kikuchi

I went to church on the streetcar and everybody was glaring at me. I couldn't figure out why. It never happened before. So then I went to church and they said Pearl Harbor was attacked. They thought it would be best to go back to our own apartments. . . . I don't know how much time elapsed between Pearl Harbor and the evacuation, but in the beginning, the church was trying to keep up with news of the evacuation, to find out any information, to keep the community together. And I was helping them from the beginning until the time of the evacuation. I was answering the church telephone, mostly because I was able to speak Japanese. Most of the old church members spoke Japanese. I kept pretty busy; I couldn't do much anything else.

Lili Sasaki

I was walking home from helping my brother-in-law in his snack shop, and I saw the newspaper on the stand: "Japan bombed Pearl Harbor." Oh, I felt terrible. My god, don't tell me such an awful thing like that! And when I got home, two FBI men came and were waiting for my father-in-law. They said they wouldn't leave until he came. My father-in-law didn't come home until about dinnertime, around seven. And the minute he came, they told him to "pack up a few things and come with us." It's because he belonged to some of those Japanese associations. He was quite well known in Japantown. And he was a writer. He had printed three books in Japan. But we didn't see him at all. We never heard from him for, I don't know, six months. We didn't know what happened.

Yeah, that was very bad. After Pearl Harbor, I just hated to go outside on the street. Then the government told you not to travel so many miles from your home. But I had to get to work. I had to make some money. And as I was going through the turnstile, a policeman stopped me and said, "What are you, are you Japanese?" And I didn't stop. I said, "No, I'm not Japanese." But I think the young policeman was too embarrassed to chase me. He let me go. But I thought I was American. I was born here, so I just said, "No." So I went to work.

Jack Matsuoka

When I heard the news of Pearl Harbor, I didn't believe it. My folks didn't believe it either. It never hit us until the army put out a curfew right in the center of Watsonville. Main Street—if you're a citizen you can cross Main Street, if not, you can't. So I had to do the shopping for my folks.

Then the FBI picked my father up. He was just nobody, but they picked him up anyhow. They came in the morning and asked where he was. I told them I didn't know. This big bruiser of an agent, a cross between a football fullback and a Nazi stormtrooper, said, "Don't get sassy with me!" He didn't call me any names, but his tone. . . . They surrounded the house; one agent came in from the rear, two came in from the front. The leader said, "Don't worry, we're going to take care of your father—you'll hear from us." Just like the movies. They took him away. It was nearly a year before we were together again.

136

Jack Matsuoka, "Well, what about this postcard with the Japanese Battleship?", pencil.

Frank Kadowaki

The FBI came around while I was on the farm. I spoke English pretty well, so they thought I was a citizen of this country. So they didn't send me to the other camp, like for spies from Japan. They didn't put me into the other camp, just the concentration camp. Otherwise they have to separate me from my family.

Yoshiko Uchida

The three of us watched Papa go down the dark hallway with the guard and disappear around a corner. He was gone, and we didn't know if we would ever see him again. There were rumors that men such as my father were to be held as hostages in reprisal for atrocities committed by the Japanese soldiers. If the Japanese killed American prisoners, it was possible my father might be among those killed in reprisal.[1]

Charles Mikami

The FBI took me over to the immigration office and the jail. I'm never against America. I'm loyal to America because my wife is born in this coun-

Gene Sogioka, FBI Takes Father Away, watercolor.

try—America—and my children are born in America. I don't do anything against America.

The hearing board says, "Well, after you came from Japan, six years later, you organized a Japanese young men's association. And you were president for five years, and when the New Year comes, Japanese put the picture of the emperor up like this."

"No, no, I don't," I say. "Young men's association doesn't pay any attention to the emperor. [They are] American-born mostly. You must mean Japanese association, first-generation association. So you made mistake." The secretaries were typing away like that. "Let me get out of here because I have to see my wife. She got a nervous breakdown!" I say. My wife can't do anything. She worry too much. Little kids. And our grocery and car, she got to sell now cheap—everything. So I worry about her every night and I couldn't sleep good. So I had to get out from here.

And they understood. A friend of mine—a lawyer from Tacoma, we go fishing together—talked to the hearing board. Maybe the hearing board telephoned to this man.

And he said, "Oh, Mikami, he's a nice man. He's all right. He's safe, I think."

And next day, jail guard comes: "Hey Mikami, you can join your family tomorrow. Prepare to go out within forty minutes."

George Akimoto

My dad was head of a couple of organizations which I guess the FBI considered dangerous or subversive. So one morning, about 7 o'clock, they broke through our front door and came in with sub-machine guns. One of the deputies—I guess the FBI had recently sworn him in—used to be a bill collector in Stockton and used to collect bills for my dad. He came in with them. They saw my Sea Scout uniform and said, "What's that?"

I said, "Can't you see the Boy Scout emblem on that?"

They questioned us, and then they said, "We're going to have to take him." They took my mother's knitting book that was written in Japanese—you know, knit one, purl two. They thought it was a code book. That was the only evidence they took when they took my old man. I could see them just running that thing through the army deciphering machine!

So they took him and put him in the local jail. This was in the wintertime. He didn't even take his topcoat because he thought he would be back in a day or two. Next thing we know, we got a letter from Bismarck, North Dakota. He's up there in a camp freezing his butt off in the snow up there without his topcoat! Eventually he wound up in Santa Fe, New Mexico, actually with prisoners of war from the European theater—Germans, Italians. Then all of a sudden, they released him and he came back to Arkansas where we were.

Lili Sasaki

Right after December 7 wherever I went I felt so self-conscious and embarrassed. I went to the library once and this handsome woman—about fifty, in a pretty dress, gray-haired, tall—looked at me and stuck her tongue out. I couldn't believe it! Then on the bus in Los Angeles, I heard two women in front of me—they knew I could hear—they were saying: "One thing is certain, we should get all the Japs, line them along the Pacific Ocean and shoot them." Two women saying that! . . . But evacuation was really a shock. At first we didn't believe it; there were rumors that we might have to be sent some 150 miles from the coast. Yes, all the time there were rumors.

And then the newspapers started writing how disloyal the Japanese were and this and that. And then they put big signs in the barber shops, "No Japs." We didn't even go to Chinese restaurants after that anymore. At first they thought just a few Japanese closest to the coast would be evacuated, but then they decided to move everybody in Los Angeles. That's why we had to hurry up and get rid of all our things. We couldn't take in any cameras, knives, books. Suddenly having to get rid of everything and being given two weeks to do it in!

You could only bring one little suitcase and handcase. They gave you the measurement—it couldn't be this big or this high. So we didn't know what to expect. We sold all our things within two weeks. Put everything out front, sold my wedding presents and furniture for fifteen cents, twenty-five cents, and went into camp. Now of course, when they told us we had to get rid of everything in two weeks, every house had to make a bonfire to burn off their junk. Then they'd say, "They're burning off all the evidence." They were accusing. Things like that. They said they built great big storage houses. The government said you could have your furniture brought there. But nobody wanted to do it—a lot of them did, but more of them didn't—because we thought they were going to confiscate it. We didn't know. . . .

Where I worked at the ceramic studio painting these cookie jars, all the artists were so disgusted because I was leaving. And I felt terrible too. One woman said, "Lili, if they're not going to treat you right, you let us know and we'll go in there." She said, "On the margin of your letter, you just write little dots or something and that means you're not being treated well."

Frank Kadowaki

A lot of people had businesses and farms. They had built up their own way, then they have to leave it—everything—where they are. My farm went back to the Irvine company. We leased. But other people, I think have a hundred, fifty, twenty-five acres of their own, they have to leave it, everything right there. You can't take furniture, or anything belonging to you. Only the clothes, whatever you got, could you use. We just take spoon and fork. Can't even take eating knife. I think they're scared for the sharp knife; they're scared cutting ourselves. They don't even give us chance to take knife. So we just take spoon and fork, that's all. . . . After the war, burglar got in and stole everything that we had left. We lost very bad.

Masao and Sada Mori

We kept our florist business until the Second World War. With Pearl Harbor, nobody buy our flowers—we want to sell them—but we have to get rid of it. That's the only way. The relocation order was a big shock. It sure was.

140

Chiura Obata, Congregation Church, April 30, 1942, ink and brush.

They hung up notices to get ready for evacuation. It said on such and such a day you go . . . so what can you do? We can't do anything. They said we had to do it, so you just do it the way they want, that's all.

We were renting a house, so we weren't able to store much. People came to buy things. We sold our furniture. Stuff like that you have to sell; you can't take it away with you. You are limited to two suitcases—what you can carry. We just took bedding, clothing. That's about all.

American Friends Service Committee Bulletin (1942)

As night of the second day of the evacuation of Terminal Island drew on and the deadline drew even nearer, little groups still toiled feverishly in an effort to load and move the last remnants of all the disrupted homes within the allotted time.

The empty houses were dark, as the electric current had been cut off. Unable to carry flashlights, which were contraband, they finished their tasks in the gleam of flashlights held steadily for hours on end in the hands of Caucasian friends who flocked to their aid.

In this area of vital defense, no light shone from factories, stores or ships —all was total darkness. But looking upward now and again, one could always pick out the same sure stars in their same sure places, and be strangely reassured. Suddenly, out of the darkness, a clear young voice said: "Well, at least, you can't black out the stars!"[2]

Hiro Mizushima

I had a feeling we had to be evacuated from California—the West Coast anyway. It was an awfully emotional sort of thing. For me, it wasn't bad, I mean, not as bad as for some of the others. I was twenty-one, my brother was a couple of years younger than I, and we were still adventurous. And we were very politically naive. I think twenty-one was the average age of the Nisei at the time. There was no way we could protest or anything like that; we didn't know how. And we didn't have any political clout anyway.

George Akimoto

After the FBI took my dad away and we were ordered to move, all the neighbors were coming over trying to buy our furniture—a dollar, dollar and a half for a chair, five dollars for a couch. We had a Chrysler, and I had a Model A Ford. I think I sold my Model A Ford for fifty bucks. That was the best I could do. And our Chrysler we sold for 150 dollars I think. It was either sell it at that price, or leave the thing. I had to go close up my dad's office, pack things. A friend of ours had a big basement in his house; he had a

Chiura Obata, "Welcome. This is your new home" (October 1, 1942), ink.

farm. So we had our stuff trucked to his farm and stored it there till the end of the war.

Jack Matsuoka

When the evacuation orders came, my first reaction was what are we going to do? How are we going to get rid of the car? I don't know why I had that reaction. Must have been crazy about cars—first learning how to drive and all that. That car was the most important thing to me, and that first struck my mind; of course, that's typical of the younger kids. I was the oldest of the family—fifteen—and I didn't know what to do. We just about gave the car away. And as for the rest of the things, we bargained them off.

All of a sudden I had all this responsibility. . . . My mother especially was worried. See, my father was already gone, picked up by the FBI.

But when we left for camp, that's when it hit me the hardest. I was just a sophomore in high school. Just at the time when I would be enjoying my high school life.

Machiye Maxine Nakamura

A few weeks back, I was idly turning the well-worn pages of my journal to write down the happenings of the day. My eyes fell upon the word evacuation. Evacuation! Curious to know what I had written those days, I thumbed through, reading several pages and the days came back to me; and I was reliving each experience, the tears, laughter, and surprise, intermingled as they were in the months of May, June, July of 1942. I remember our empty green house as we were leaving it, our going out of town, past the graveyard where our loved ones lay buried, perhaps luckily, I thought. I wanted to cry, but could not. I wanted to cry to show my love for what I was leaving, but the tears would not come. It seemed if they fell at all, they were dry tears.[3]

12

Gene Sogioka

When the war started, oh, they were shooting like crazy in California! They panicked; they didn't know what was going on around there. In San Pedro, they have this army station. What do you think they were shooting at? Just a piece of balloon. And the next day, the *Los Angeles Examiner*, it said, we shot a Japanese jet bomber! You know, it's crazy!

And the worst part is, when Pearl Harbor happened, they have this investigation. Anybody that went to Japan in the last two years, the FBI will come right there and investigate. You know what the FBI looked like in those days? They wore black hats, funny-looking things, long brim like that— stupid-looking things! You've seen them on TV today. In those days, if you are head of a social Japanese association, Chamber of Commerce, or something like that, the FBI would pick you up.

The people who lived along the Pacific, in certain areas—Seattle, or San Francisco, or Terminal Island—they have only twenty-four hours to evacuate, because the people think these are all spies. They are fishermen mostly.

We had to evacuate. If I stayed in Covina, where I was living then, I would have to have gone right away to Santa Anita. My father said, "We're going to go to the Santa Anita camp, stay with all our friends." I said, "No. We're going to move to Fresno. As long as we have a chance to stay free, until they say we got to go to camp, we're not going."

One October day in 1982, in the well-worn living room of his modest home in Larchmont, New York, Gene Sogioka, beer in one hand, cigarette in the other, spoke unhesitatingly of his evacuation experience. An old, deaf dog nuzzled us before lying down at our feet; a cat slept before a space heater. Outgoing and personable, the sixty-nine-year-old Sogioka seemed to relish the opportunity to relieve some of the solitude of his relatively recent retirement. His excitement over our discovery of his Poston watercolors at Cornell University was undeniable. He studied the photographs we had brought with us intently, as if mentally trying to leap back into that long-ago, yet hardly forgotten time, "Yup, that's what they looked like," he muttered again and again. On emerging from his memories, he sprang back to life to give us a private showing of his recent watercolors, the product of occasional vacations in Jamaica. Sogioka obviously likes people; it did not take long for us to warm to him. In a short time we were friends and were settling in to hear his life story.

My wife comes from near Fresno in zone 2; zone 2 is not considered evacuation right away. So, I packed up the whole house in a truck and went to Fresno. Stayed there until we moved to Sanger, which is still free zone—the other side of the highway.

I didn't have any problem because we had a twenty-acre farm. We put everything in the barn. The neighbor, Mr. Doyle, an Irishman, my father knew for sixty years. Mr. Doyle took care of the whole place. In those days [you heard], you know, "Kill the Jap! Kill the Jap!" Oh, my god! But he took care of it. He took care of the truck, the farm. He farmed it himself with his kid. He rented the house. This is the reason you don't make a friend with just anybody. You've got to know who you are, who he is. In the meantime, on my wife's side—they lived in Fresno—the whole house was burned down. They had somebody take care of the whole place; there's no alternative. Somebody rented the house or whatever, and burned the whole house down.

It's a hard thing to say, whether it's right or wrong to have to go to camp. Already right after Pearl Harbor there were people carrying guns, looking for the Japs. What good is it when you're shot? The Chinese themselves went around wearing little badges that said, "I'm American Chinese." I couldn't tell the difference between the Chinese, Koreans, Japanese. I couldn't tell the difference. But *they* made the difference. They put the badges on. I felt it's for safety. It's dangerous in those days. The people were so panicked, confused. They didn't know what to do. I thought it's better off just to go; it's for our own safety. My family, my wife's family, nobody got shot. But people did. That's what the government said, it's for our own protection.

Also, there's nothing you can do. It's the same sort of situation like when you're drafted into the army. You just have to go.

Before the evacuation I was just trying to make something. I wanted to do

146

something. My father was a farmer. We had a twenty-acre farm. Get up at five o'clock in the morning, plow the fields, work like that. I decided I didn't want to farm. I decided to go to college. I went to two years at Pomona College. But I hear about these people who go to college, get a degree, and then can't get a job. The Japanese people finally have the money to send their kids to college. But when you get out of college in those days, there's no job because of what they call prejudice. They will not hire Japanese. So we end up working in the fruit markets or something like that. So I said, "The heck with that." That's what happened. So I said, "I quit." I decided I was going to be a real professional, and I went to art school.

I thought it would be more professional. It's hard, I mean. . . . Do you have talent? Do you? You don't know. But you've got to try it, someway. That's what I felt when I was young.

So I decided, and I went to Chouinard Art School, and worked and worked. I was considered one of the three best artists in my class. When I left Chouinard, I decided to go to Disney. I worked as a background artist for *Fantasia*, *Dumbo*, and *Bambi*. The picture I worked on real hard is *Dumbo*. [Disney] was a man of imagination. We all have imagination. You have to have imagination. You have to create something. That's how I feel even today. If you don't have the imagination, creativity, you're dead.

I got married in 1939. Her name is Mini; she's a Nisei. Her real Japanese name is Miné. But when they registered us to Fresno County Clerk, they mistook it for Mini. My real Japanese name is Isao. Somebody mistook it in our Covina High School yearbook for Isaac! Yeah. When the war started I had a year-old daughter.

I didn't start that war. Shit! I didn't start the war. But what can I do? They put us in the camp. You can't *do* anything in the camp—no painting, no nothing. The thing is you have to make the best of it in the camp. I wasn't carrying any chip on my shoulder against the government or anything. No. It's the condition; you have to get used to it. My father and mother were in there for three years.

When we entered Poston, we were only allowed a seventy-five-pound or something dufflebag. I still have it upstairs. It has a number on it. You don't go by the name at that time, just a number. My wife carried seventy-five pounds. My father, my mother, my brother—each carried seventy-five pounds. [When we first arrived in the desert] all I saw was the watertank. This is one thing I could never forget, because it was so hot and we had to sit and wait, because there were only three buses to take us to Poston from the train station twenty miles away at Parker. I remember the day was hot and there was water dripping down our backs.

Gene Sogioka, The Loneliness of Poston, watercolor.

You have no idea. In the first place, Poston, the camp was on an Indian reservation near the Colorado River. There were no Indians. It's just empty land. Nothing. And there was mesquite wood all over the place. And everything was exposed. There were rattlesnakes as big as this! We built the whole thing. We grew everything—vegetables and all this and that. But you wouldn't like to live there. Camp was something like an army camp. Just barracks, tar-papered barracks. We didn't have guard towers. We didn't have barbed wire fence. But the other camps had, I've seen pictures. But as far as I'm concerned, Poston, Arizona—102 degrees in the summertime with the dust coming up—I don't think any other camp was like that. I think we had the worst camp.

At first, there was no bed in the barracks. So they brought in a big truck with dry hay. They dump the whole thing of hay at the front of Block 222. They give you a mattress bag. We got to pick up all the hay, put it in a bag and make a mattress. There was no bed. I had to put in on the floor, tempo-

rarily I guess. But the thing is, the floor is not covered. You got a quarter inch in between the boards. And you have 115, 120 degree heat and a dust storm. That dust storm comes up like crazy! Then about six to eight months later they decided they are going to give us linoleum to cover the floor. I put that whole thing in myself. Later on, I built a bed, put a curtain up.

The camp was self-governing. All the vegetables we grew ourselves. The only thing the government provided is food like the meat, bread, the rice. The Japanese are farmers, they grow everything in the desert. My father worked in the adobe section, making adobe blocks, bricks. We built the whole school. That's what we did. We didn't ask anybody to build a school. We did it ourselves.

When the first evacuees came to the relocation camp—they are from Terminal Island, mostly from Los Angeles, and they move into Poston #1—these Arizonians, a truckload of men with shotguns, travel from Parker to the camp. They're going to shoot them (the evacuees) all. So, it's a good thing they had a MP; he stopped them.

Also, they have in those days, at Tucson, Arizona, a World War II airplane basic training unit. Well, over the camp, this guy comes on like he is going to bomb us or something. They hate us. Fly down right over the camp. Finally we complained. And finally the administration called up and said, "You've got to stop that. This is not an enemy camp."

During the first week, I found it difficult to get a job. And naturally you wanted a job so badly. . . . The only thing I could get was a job to help in the kitchen. This was not a regular salary job. This was voluntary. I served two weeks volunteering washing dishes. Then I was working for Dr. Leighton

150

Gene Sogioka, After the Show, 1942, watercolor.

[Alexander Leighton, sociologist/psychiatrist studying the camp]; I just paint and I just exhibit. I didn't even know where the paintings went. I didn't know, until you called me up and I found out. A forty-year surprise!

I sketched everything about the camp: the people, the conditions. Dr. Leighton didn't tell me what to paint. I'm not that type. I just paint, sketch, show to him. That's the way it works. I went around and sketched the conditions, landscapes.

There was an exhibit at Cambridge, Mass. A painting of mine, "Duststorm" won honorable mention at that exhibit. I think I got the prize because they can feel it—102 degrees in the summertime and when that damn dust-storm starts, holy smokes! You have no idea. They gave me honorable mention because of the feeling. When you paint something, you have to put in your feelings; express yourself. That's what I think. Picasso, when he paints an apple, he's not going to paint that thing with the highlights so if some-

151

body comes to see it they say they could touch it. He paints a feeling of it. It's a creation. That's what you're doing. You have to create something! You have to be different. If you're going to paint something just to see what it looks like—like a photograph—there's no sense painting it.

Also in camp, I taught art in the school. In Camp 2 I painted the whole Buddhist shrine: the lilies, flowers, the wall, curtains in the Buddhist church. In Camp 2, they had an outdoor stage, and there was a play going on once a month or something like that there. I painted the curtain, a big one. This is after they have the show. They had movies too; government provides the movies. Everybody takes chairs. Enjoys. That's the only thing you could do.

The problems in the camps came from what they called the age gap. In

152

Gene Sogioka, Poston Strike Rally, watercolor.

the camp they had a struggle between young and old. One of the young people says, "The hell with it; I can't stay in this camp," and they just take off. They volunteer for the army.

But the old man Issei says, "No, the government took us to the relocation camp like this. We're going to go back to Japan." Oh, then they had a fight! And it's not just the age gap, it's culture. There are two different cultures in the camp: the Nisei, and the Issei and Kibei. It's a hard thing. I'm right in the middle. What can I do? And then, they have—I think it's the most important part of the whole camp situation—the government published pamphlets which asked two questions: "Are you loyal to the United States?" and "Will you bear arms to fight for your country?" Oh, this is the big issue. Oh,

153

boy! Most people, Issei, say, "Why should you say 'yes'? The government put us in the camp." But what can the Nisei do?

You can't go around speaking your views openly because this Kibei will come out there in the middle of the night and grab you and cut your hair off. He shaved the whole hair off of the Nisei. Yes, I guess my wife was always worried about that. She said, "Don't go out there in the middle of the night."

Dr. Leighton used to come up in his Navy uniform with the lieutenant stripes on it to visit me at lunchtime. He sat next to me eating lunch. All the people look at me and call me a dog. [The Issei and Kibei] think that I'm supposed to be an agent or something because Dr. Leighton was in a uniform and comes in and talks to me or something. Then this guy, old timer, comes in and says, "How do you write your last name?" He says, "When Japan conquers the whole United States, when they're going to win the war, you'll be in the first ones going to be hanged!"

In the meantime, this old man, making that kind of statement, what do you think his son does? His son volunteers for the army—went to Italy. The Issei was up and down, crying. He's going around camp apologizing to older people—"Why did my son do a thing like that?" Apologizing to other people. I said, "No, it's not wrong. He has his own opinion. He has a right to live his own way." Oh when I saw that. . . .

We're in the same boat, that's what I'm trying to tell these people. We're in the same boat. Why can't we work together? Oh, some radical people!

One time, they had an incident. They had a big protest, something about food. That was in Camp 1; I was in Camp 2. Camp 1 is early evacuees from Terminal Island. They have a strong group of Isseis, pro-Japan; a group in the middle, like I am; and a third group who don't care, never get involved. They're fighting each other because one has the power or wants it. They had a big strike. See this flag over here? These are groups of Kibei—pro-Japan. They're having a rally.

Some people want to elect me for the block manager. But I don't want to. It's not worth it. I didn't want to be involved. So much political party fighting.

We go fishing in the Colorado River. I like fishing; I still do today. A lot of Japanese people like fishing. It's the only place you could relax—fishing or something like that in the Colorado. Walked four miles through all the mesquite wood and the rattlesnakes. And this guy—this is very important —this representative from California named [John M.] Costello, he's on what they call in those days the Dies Committee. He comes to the camp; it was his order to see what goes on there, I suppose. Well, he finds a piece of Wonderbread bag on the riverbank where we were fishing. So you use a little bread for bait, that's it. This Costello made a report. He said that Japanese

were waiting for a submarine coming up the Colorado River! I don't think it's funny; it's crazy!

Even today I think why didn't they put the Italians and the Germans in the camps? But the point is the majority of the population is Italians and Germans and you can't do that to the population. Because we are a minority. . . .

Some say we shouldn't be in relocation camps. We are American citizens. I don't feel like that. The conditions we were in with the war and this and that. . . . You can't carry a chip on your shoulder.

It's wrong. I mean it's wrong in the black and white, what you write on the piece of paper. Unconstitutional. But when you talk about how you feel about it, I really don't know. It's something else. I really don't know.

Biographical Sketches

George Akimoto

At the time of the evacuation order, George Akimoto had finished one and a half years of junior college in his hometown of Stockton, California. In late 1941, Akimoto and a friend had volunteered for the navy. Then came Pearl Harbor, and although Akimoto had been accepted into the navy, he was never summoned for induction because of his Japanese ancestry. His friend, a Caucasian, was on the first ship to go down in the Pacific.

Instead, Akimoto's family was forced from its home and interned at the Stockton fairgrounds and then at the relocation camp at Rohwer, Arkansas. "It got me out of a small town at least," he told us with characteristic good humor.

While at the Stockton assembly center, Akimoto took over the job of art editor of the camp newspaper. He later had the same job on the *Rohwer Outpost* and in that capacity created the cartoon character who cavorted through the pages of every issue of the *Outpost* and who was to become the camp's mascot: L'il Dan'l. Looking like a stereotypical "Nip" but sporting a coonskin cap and other Arkansas "boonie" accoutrements, L'il Dan'l "showed us the humor and ironies in the trivial things that have happened to us," Akimoto wrote in a camp one-year anniversary booklet he compiled in 1943.

Akimoto left Rohwer for New York City, where he secured his first job in a commercial art studio. He has since returned to California and is a successful commercial artist in the Los Angeles area.

"I look at these forty years later, and it's the same feeling," Hisako Hibi said as she placed a few of her many camp oil paintings against the walls of her small San Francisco Japantown apartment. "The flowers in the painting from Topaz are sunflowers. Only the sunflowers grew in the desert. We didn't have any other flowers. . . ."

Hibi was born in Japan and came to the United States with her parents when she was fourteen years old. She studied Western-style oil painting at the California School of Fine Arts (now the San Francisco Art Institute) and exhibited her work throughout the area. In 1942 she was sent to the Tanforan assembly center with her husband, son, and daughter Ibuki. "My husband and I were born in Japan and were told that we were unnaturalized enemy aliens; so that we have to endure whatever the condition it might be. But for our children five and ten years old and all other Japanese American children born in U.S.A., it was their future we were concerned about the most," she wrote in 1976.

Hibi was involved in the formation of the Tanforan and Topaz art schools. After three and a half years of confinement, the Hibis went to New York. When her husband died in 1947, Hibi was forced many times to put away her brushes and work as a housekeeper, dressmaker, and factory hand to make a living. She was granted U.S. citizenship in 1953 and later returned to San Francisco. A member of San Francisco Women Artists and Perception Gallery, she has often exhibited her camp art and her more recent paintings.

George Matsusaburo Hibi

George Matsusaburo Hibi was born in Japan on June 21, 1886. He attended grammar school, high school, and law school in Japan. In 1906 he immigrated to the United States where he settled first in San Francisco and then in Hayward, California. He was a self-taught artist until 1919, when he enrolled in the California School of Fine Arts in San Francisco. A prolific exhibitor, he was also a cartoonist for various newspapers and an organizer of several art societies. In 1930 he married Hisako and subsequently had two children. He died of cancer in New York City in 1947.

Hibi wrote from camp for the 1945 San Francisco Art Association exhibit: "I am now inside of barbed wires but still sticking in Art—I seek no dirt of the Earth—but the light of the star of the sky."

Hibi's thoughts on the World War II evacuation and relocation in this text have been excerpted from various documents in the Japanese American Research Project collection at UCLA.

Yonekichi Hosoi

Eiko Katayama, a retired computer programmer analyst living in Berkeley, California, and her husband shared her father's unique World War II internment drawings with us. Hosoi was born in Tokyo in 1884 and immigrated to the United States in 1902. He attended the California College of Arts and Crafts, and before the war had an embroidery shop where he made his own designs. He died in 1951.

Some of his drawings were in the traditional sumi style (Japanese watercolor), other were illustrations of Utai drama and Japanese fairy tales. Most noteworthy were a series of drawings, one for each block in Topaz, illustrating a unique aspect of that block, accompanied by a philosophical poem/prayer for peace.

Estelle Ishigo

Hundreds of pencil sketches, watercolors, and oil paintings by Estelle Ishigo are housed in the University of California at Los Angeles library. Just before the evacuation, Ishigo, the Caucasian wife of Arthur Shigeharu Ishigo, a Californian of Japanese ancestry, had begun work as a teacher at the Hollywood Art Center. After two weeks of employment, she was told to leave because the students and their parents would object to her Japanese name. Having no money to travel together out of the military area, Estelle Ishigo found herself forced to evacuate with her husband. She followed him to the Pomona assembly center and then the relocation center at Heart Mountain, Wyoming, where they lived for three years. For much of that time, she worked as an artist for the War Relocation Authority Reports Division at the evacuee salary of nineteen dollars a month. Her book *Lone Heart Mountain*, written in camp, presents one of the acerbic accounts of the internment. Estelle Ishigo's camp art has been exhibited throughout California.

Frank Kadowaki

Frank Kadowaki was born in the seaside town of Shimane, Japan. He immigrated to the United States in the early 1900s, when he was eighteen years old: "When I was eight years old, my mother left me in Japan and came to the United States to join my father. So I didn't even see my father's face until I was eighteen." He joined his parents on their farm in Santa Ana, California.

Although he had studied fine arts at the Otis Art Institute in Los Angeles, after marrying he found himself farming to make a living. Until the war started he leased land from the Irvine Ranch Company.

After three years in Poston, the Kadowaki family relocated to New York, first to work for a family in Port Jervis and then to work in Oriental art restoration at the Metropolitan Museum of Art. Frank Kadowaki since has moved back to California, where he and his wife run an Asian art and antique shop in the Pacific Asia Museum in Pasadena. They have two sons and a daughter.

Atsushi Kikuchi

Reserved, modest, and somewhat hesitant to talk to us, Atsushi Kikuchi, we came to find out, was an introspective man. His words were carefully chosen, his remarks insightful, his story complete.

Kikuchi is Kibei: born in Seattle, he spent most of his childhood in Japan before returning to the United States. He told us he always liked to draw, so when he won a scholarship to the California College of Arts and Crafts, he found himself with an opportunity he could not pass up. Since he was one of ten children, any kind of opportunity was all right with his parents; they neither encouraged nor discouraged him from entering the art profession, Kikuchi told us. Nonetheless, he calls himself "the black sheep of the whole family—the only one without a college degree."

At the time of Pearl Harbor, he was in his early twenties and living alone in Los Angeles. He was interned at Santa Anita and then at Amache, Colorado. After a fairly short stay at Amache, Kikuchi was able to relocate to Chicago and then was inducted into the U.S. Army, where he was trained in the intelligence division. He was stationed in Japan as part of the occupation force. Today he lives with his family in Chicago, where he does freelance advertising work.

Jack Matsuoka

Jack Matsuoka, a Nisei living in the San Francisco area, is a successful political cartoonist and the author of *Camp II, Block 211*, a collection of sketches he did while interned at Poston.

He was born in 1925 and grew up in the farming city of Watsonville, California. A natural scribbler, Matsuoka drew long before he was interned. He left for Poston when he was seventeen—"just at the time when I would have been enjoying my high school life." His cartoons illustrate the teenager's experience in camp. Their lighthearted style effectively captures the irony of camp life.

160

In 1944, Matsuoka was able to go to Cleveland to work for a lumber company. He enrolled in the Cleveland School of Fine Arts, but after one semester was drafted into the army and was soon stationed in Japan. He eventually returned to California, married, and had two daughters. He has authored additional books and works as a cartoonist for numerous publications.

Charles (Suiko) Mikami

Charles (Suiko) Mikami was born in December 1901 at Saijo-machi, Hiroshima-ken, Japan. At the age of fourteen he began studying Japanese "sumi-e" painting. After graduating from school in 1919, he came to the United States and settled in Seattle. For a while he worked there as a sumi-e instructor, but the Depression changed his plans. He found he needed to make a living some other way. "So I quit. I stop teaching and painting— twenty-nine years old. I got to work hard." He worked as a truck driver for farmers.

Immediately after Pearl Harbor, Mikami was detained and questioned by the FBI, but he was quickly released and allowed to join his wife and children at the Pinedale assembly center. Subsequently he was interned at Tule Lake and then at Topaz. He occupied himself by teaching art, painting, and playing sports.

When the Japanese were allowed to return to the West Coast at the end of the war, Mikami and his family moved to Morgan Hill, California, just south of San Jose, to farm. He owned and operated a fruit stand along the highway there until his retirement in 1972. He has been and is still actively involved in community service, demonstrating sumi painting to school, church, and community groups, and devoting much time to the San Francisco Senryu poem study group. For his civic service and particularly for his contribution to Japanese-American friendship and cultural exchange, the Japanese government awarded him the Order of Sacred Treasure, Fifth Class, in 1977. His Tule Lake and Topaz paintings are now housed at the California First Bank's Japanese American History Room in San Francisco.

Hiro Mizushima

At the time of Pearl Harbor, Hiro Mizushima was living with his father and brother in what he called the "Oriental Ghetto" of Oakland, California. At home he spoke Japanese: "My dad taught in the Japanese school." He was attending the California College of Arts and Crafts. When ordered to evacuate, the family moved to the free zone around Lodi, where his parents had farmed earlier.

After three months, they were ordered interned as well, and went to the Stockton assembly center and the Rohwer relocation camp. There, Mizushima had his first experience with commercial art; he began working for the camp newspaper and served as co-art editor of the *Rohwer Outpost*. With an irrepressible spirit he told us, "Camp wasn't all that bad—I wouldn't have met my wife!"

In May 1943, Mizushima left for Chicago where he worked and attended art school before being drafted into the army. Sent to Europe just as hostilities subsided, he made the most of his situation and enrolled in art school in Biarritz, France.

He later returned to Chicago where he eventually became vice president and graphic designer with the advertising firm of Grant, Jacoby, Inc. Now retired and living in San Marcos, California, Mizushima told us he devotes his time to the fine arts.

Masao Mori

Masao Mori was born in Japan and immigrated to the San Francisco Bay area in 1912. He had dreams of becoming a fine artist but realized it was next to impossible to make a living. Instead, he became a florist, opening his own shop in Oakland at the age of nineteen. In 1931 Mori married a Nisei, Sada. Because of the Cable Act of 1922, which stated that an American citizen who married a person not eligible for citizenship (i.e., an Asian) would lose his or her citizenship, she lost her citizenship. "It was quite a shock. They had some crazy laws back then," Sada Mori told us.

Another shock was the evacuation order, which forced them to close their florist shop and sell or store their personal belongings. Their children, then eight and ten, were a source of worry. Interned in Topaz, Masao worked as a cook; Sada as a block nurse. Mori had plenty of time to draw, however, and he painted hundreds of oil paintings: "I can't find a lot of my sketches. I put them down in the basement and. . . ."

The Moris returned to California as soon as they could after the war. "I was not worried to come back to California. I'm afraid of nothing," Masao Mori told us. They moved back to their old neighborhood in Oakland and bought the house where they live to this day. Mori began cultivating bonsai trees; their backyard teems with thousands. "That's why now I don't draw —no sketching, no drawing. These bonsai grow so we can't leave them alone. If you don't take care the shape is spoiled. So I do that in the daytime. I like it. The bonsai is art too, just a little different," he said.

Chiura Obata

Chiura Obata arrived in San Francisco from Japan in 1906. Then eighteen years old, he was about to be drafted into the Japanese army. Instead he planned to go to Europe to study painting; his father had been a painter too. On the way, he went to California and found the landscape intriguing, Yosemite and the High Sierras in particular. He decided to stay. From 1931 to 1957, he was a professor of art at the University of California, Berkeley, a tenure interrupted by his detention at Tanforan and Topaz.

Professor Obata was instrumental in inspiring much of the art created during and preserved since the World War II internment. Not only did he himself, an established artist, depict camp life—its inhabitants, its conditions, and its creations—but he also was responsible for organizing the art schools at Tanforan and Topaz. Using his university connections he had art materials shipped into the camps. He organized those of his former Berkeley students who were interned with him into a highly skilled corps of art teachers and encouraged them to continue their own art work. He believed that everyone should record his or her unique experiences and then hold on to those creations as a record for future generations.

Obata, who was considered ardently "pro-America," met with some trouble in Topaz. One night an internee who disagreed with his politics hit him with an iron pipe in the bathhouse, and he was rushed to a hospital in Salt Lake City. His family followed him there and they subsequently resettled in St. Louis, where they lived until 1949. The Obatas then returned to Berkeley.

Chiura Obata died in 1975 after leading a distinguished and full life that included receiving the Kungoto Zuihose Medal from the emperor of Japan in 1965 and publishing many art books. His wife, Haruko, now in her nineties, is active in the Berkeley community, where she teaches flower arranging. She and her daughter, Mrs. Yuri Kodani, shared their camp memories and Professor Obata's sketches and paintings with us.

Miné Okubo

Miné Okubo was born in Riverside, California, in 1912 into a poor family of seven children. She attended Riverside Junior College from 1933 to 1934 and was encouraged by a professor there to go to the University of California at

163

Berkeley to study art. After receiving both her B.A. and M.A., she won a traveling fellowship to study in Europe. Eighteen months later the outbreak of fighting there forced her to return to California, where she found work through the Federal Arts Project doing mosaic murals for the army in Oakland. World War II intervened again, and she was interned at Tanforan and later Topaz.

In 1944, *Fortune* magazine brought her out of camp to help illustrate their special issue on Japan, and Okubo decided to make New York her home. In 1946, Columbia University Press published *Citizen 13660*, her account of camp life (recently reissued in a revised edition by the University of Washington Press). After a number of years working as a freelance illustrator, Okubo decided to devote her time solely to fine art. She has had numerous one-woman and group shows.

Siberius Y. Saito

On December 29, 1908, Siberius Y. Saito was born on the ship carrying his mother and father to America from Japan. Because he was born between Hawaii and San Francisco, he was considered an American citizen. He never traveled to Japan, but he loved Japanese things, Saito's sister, K. Ruth Saito, told us. He was trained as an architect. "Since childhood he had always sketched a lot," she explained. "It was automatic. In his teens, he started sketching from movie magazines." His widely exhibited pencil sketches of the Tanforan assembly center have both the trained architect's objectivity and a fine artist's subjectivity. He worked at Tanforan teaching art and architecture.

Saito helped in the initial site planning of the Topaz center and was also an art instructor. Soon after his arrival at Topaz, he left to practice architecture in Madison, Wisconsin. There he met his future partner; the two formed the firm of Flinn and Saito in Waterloo, Iowa, where Saito lived and worked until his death in 1980.

Lili Yuri Sasaki

When her daughter was born at the start of the 1940s, Lili Yuri Sasaki decided to stay near her parents in Los Angeles until her husband finished his medical internship in Ohio; he could not earn enough to support a family. She worked meanwhile in a ceramics studio that made cookie jars. Pearl Harbor was to present a new challenge. She told us that although she could have gone immediately to Cincinnati to rejoin her husband, she decided instead to have an investigative adventure—deliberately to go into camp. With an intelligence, articulateness, and effervescence that persist to this day, Sasaki weathered life in Santa Anita and Amache well, always doing something—teaching art, organizing social events—while always staying aware. After a year's stay, she went to join her husband. In 1975, the Sasakis moved back to California, to Berkeley, where they are retired.

Lawrence Sasano

Living on his own in Los Angeles from an early age, Lawrence Sasano learned to be resourceful. He studied advertising and advertising photography at the Art Center in Los Angeles and was doing freelance photography when the exclusion order was signed. "I was three decades and one when I went to Poston, but I'll say I had a better life than the average person because of my attitude and because of how I was able to cope with it. I did the best under the circumstances," he told us. Because Sasano had been an avid naturalist, he was well prepared for the rigors of Poston life, and he was able to use his naturalistic and artistic skills to help make Poston less dreary for many young people.

After nine and a half months Sasano left Poston to join the army's airborne division, flying over the jungles of the South Pacific. He was with the occupation forces in Japan. "When the war ended I made up my mind I was coming back and going to do something worthwhile for the young people," he said. "That's how I became involved in the Boy Scouts as a volunteer. I've been a trainer of trainers. I have received all the highest awards that you could possibly receive." He is still active in scouting and lives with his wife in Los Angeles.

Yoriyuki Sato

Sato and his wife were teachers in Japan. When they immigrated to California in the early 1900s, they started out as farmers, one of the few jobs available to them at the time. They later moved to Pasadena, and became florists. They were evacuated first to the Tulare assembly center, then to the Gila River relocation camp. Their son, Dr. George Sato of St. Louis, told us, "In camp, this was the first time we had a semblance of family life because my parents finally had time to spend with us. Their artistic talents didn't come out until the camp because they were too busy working; my mother always wanted them to work harder in the florist shop. Art was not done for a livelihood."

Nancy Sato has saved the paintings her grandfather did in camp. She said the only time Yoriyuki Sato, who recently died, painted was when he was interned. His paintings have the honesty of someone expessing himself in a new medium.

Gene Sogioka

Born in California, but, like many eldest sons of Japanese immigrants, raised in Japan with relatives, Sogioka returned to America when he was fourteen years old. In 1938, after studying fine and commercial art at Chouinard Art Institute in Los Angeles, he worked under Millard Sheets on a large mural at the San Francisco Exposition. In the years immediately preceding Pearl Harbor, Sogioka taught art part-time and began working full-time as a background artist for Walt Disney Studios.

Sogioka, his wife, and their very young daughter were among the second group transported to the Poston camp. Sogioka had some of his watercolors with him. The attention these attracted got him a job that not only gave him a new perspective on the evacuation and internment, but also allowed him to do what he liked to do: paint. The Bureau of Sociological Research, under the direction of Lieutenant Alexander H. Leighton, a sociologist and psychiatrist with the navy's research division, had been set up to observe camp life and to study the effects of the evacuation on the internees. (Leighton's conclusions are in his 1945 book, *The Governing of Men.*) Leighton hired Sogioka at evacuee wages to document in pictures the life of the evacuees. He was to describe with brush and pigment what the others in the bureau were describing in words.

After a few years in camp, Sogioka went to New York City, where he worked as a commercial artist until his retirement in 1979. He has three married daughters and grandchildren.

Henry Sugimoto

Born in Wakayama, Japan, in 1901, Henry Sugimoto emigrated in 1919 to join his parents in Hanford, California. "Back when I was a small boy I like very much to draw, and my grandfather encouraged me. Whenever I make a drawing, my grandfather says, 'Oh, that's wonderful!' and shows my relatives, you know, and that makes me proud," he told us.

166

He went to Hanford High School and upon graduation enrolled at the University of California at Berkeley, but later transferred to the California College of Arts and Crafts. "I agreed to go to the University of California, so I started going to academic courses at the university. But I don't like science, and I have to take astronomy and zoology. One day, my friend came to university and asked me to visit California College of Art. So one day I went to art school with him. After one semester, I think I changed to art school." He received his B.F.A. in 1928. In 1929 he left for Paris, where he studied at the Academie Coroasrossi and exhibited at the Salon d'Automne.

When he returned to the United States, he married and had a daughter. He continued his painting, exhibiting in many galleries and museums. Then with World War II, Sugimoto and his family found themselves interned at the Fresno assembly center and later at the Jerome and Rohwer relocation centers in Arkansas. During his confinement, he taught art in high school and in the evenings.

After the camps closed, the Sugimotos moved to New York City, where they met with hard times. Sugimoto illustrated books and translated movie captions into Japanese before landing a job designing fabric. He worked for the fabric company until 1962, by which time he had saved enough money to devote his time to fine arts. He has published a book of his camp life paintings in Japan, has been honored by the emperor with a medal for his contribution to Japanese culture in America, and has received several medals from the Japanese government for his contribution to art. In 1984, Sugimoto donated some of his camp art to the permanent collection of the Smithsonian National Museum of American History.

Kango Takamura

Kango Takamura was born in Japan in January 1895 and immigrated to Hawaii when he was seventeen years old. He spent ten years there and then left for the mainland because he had become interested in the new motion picture industry. After a short stay in the New York offices of Paramount Studios, he moved to Hollywood. At the time of Pearl Harbor he was working as a photo retoucher for RKO Studios in Los Angeles. He was detained by the FBI at Santa Fe, New Mexico, and then was released and allowed to join his wife, daughter, son-in-law and granddaughter at Manzanar. After leaving Manzanar, he returned to Hollywood and worked at RKO Studios for another twenty-five years before retiring. Since then he has been a very active church member and as he told us, "enjoying so much my life in America."

Tokutaro (Kakunen) Tsuruoka

Mrs. Haruno Tsuruoka, proprietor of Daruma Art Framing Store and Gallery in New York, told us of her father-in-law, Tokutaro Tsuruoka. He had arrived in San Francisco when he was "in his early teens. His life was full of art. He was an oriental antique dealer. Art had always been his avocation." Interned at Poston, in Camp III, he supervised all artisan activities. "He didn't like to paint the camp. He would go out very early in the morning into the desert and foothills surrounding the camp to paint. His paintings are very romantic. He really caught the sense of loneliness, but he saw beauty even under such circumstance." He died in 1977 at the age of eighty-five.

Yoshiko Uchida

When Yoshiko Uchida learned of the evacuation orders, she was a senior at the University of California at Berkeley. She had spent her entire life in Berkeley. She, her older sister, and her Issei mother were interned first at Tanforan, then at Topaz. Her father, who had been arrested by the FBI, joined them after his release from the Department of Justice camp in Missoula, Montana.

To make constructive use of otherwise idle time, Uchida took art classes. Her first attempts garnered her second prize in a camp art exhibit. She also taught second grade at the camp's school. Like many young men and women, Uchida left Topaz through the National Student Relocation Council's program, to attend Smith College on a full graduate fellowship. She later moved to New York, then traveled to Japan as a Ford Foundation Fellow, and eventually resettled in Berkeley.

Uchida is the author of more than two dozen children's books, including *Journey to Topaz* and *Journey Home*. Her most recent book for adults is *Desert Exile*, a vivid and intense account of her incarceration.

Masao Yabuki

"When the evacuation happened I was still going to school. They sent my degree to Tanforan," Masao Yabuki told us. He was working toward his masters degree in art at the University of California, Berkeley. Incarcerated at Tanforan and Topaz, Yabuki found himself with other artist colleagues from Berkeley, and he taught in the art school under the direction of Professor Obata. "I would set up a still life on a blackboard. I'd tell them, this is not what you see in one perspective. It is from different perspectives—from left, middle, right. Such vision isn't a photographic representation, but it tells you a better story." Yabuki held onto many of his students' works, some of which appear in this text.

Yabuki left Topaz in 1944 to look for a job. He lived in Philadelphia, working in an industrial design office, before returning to his native California.

Harry Yoshizumi

Harry Yoshizumi had just graduated from high school and was living with his family in Watsonville, California, when Roosevelt signed Executive Order 9066. "I was just thinking about maybe going to art school," he told us from his San Jose home. So while interned at Poston, Yoshizumi painted "hundreds" of watercolors. "That's all I did out there, every day." He worked in the recreation department, teaching drawing classes, designing and printing Christmas cards, trying to make the camp more liveable. He and fellow artist Gus Nakagawa designed a twenty-foot-long mural for the camp library, showing their impressions of camp life. "It covered one side wall and took us six months of working every day after library hours."

Yoshizumi stayed in Poston until the camp was about to close. In 1945 he went to New York to study art. From there he returned to California, where he became an active member of the Carmel Art Association. He hoped to become a professional artist, but in 1960 he "came to the conclusion it's not a stable life." Today he works for IBM.

Notes

We have employed the following abbreviations:

Cornell: Japanese American Relocation Center Records. Ithaca: Cornell University Libraries Department of Manuscripts and University Archives.

UCLA: Japanese American Research Project Collection. Los Angeles: The University Library, UCLA Department of Special Collections.

WRA Records: Records of the War Relocation Authority. Washington, D.C.: National Archives Building.

Shikataganai

1. Congressman John Rankin, Miss., as quoted in *The Seattle Post-Intelligencer*, February 19, 1942.

2. *Korematsu v. United States*, 323 U.S. 214 (1944) (Black, J.).

3. Earl Warren, U.S. Congress, House Select Committee Investigating National Defense Migration Hearings (Washington, D.C., 1942).

4. Nyogen Sensaki, untitled poem, UCLA.

5. Matsusaburo Hibi, "History and Development of the Topaz Art School," UCLA.

6. "Keep the Japs Out," *Los Angeles Examiner* editorial, September 29, 1943.

7. Anonymous, "Out of the Desert" (Poston, Ariz., 1940s), Cornell.

8. Machiye Maxine Nakamura, "How Evacuation Affected Me," Japanese American War Relocation Collection (Berkeley: The Bancroft Library, University of California).

9. *Los Angeles Evening Herald Express* editorial, November 9, 1943.

History I: Executive Order 9066

1. War Relocation Authority pamphlet, "Questions and Answers for Evacuees" (1942), WRA Records.

2. War Relocation Authority pamphlet (1940s), WRA Records.

Pioneer Communities

1. War Relocation Authority pamphlet, "Questions and Answers for Evacuees" (1942), WRA Records.
2. Toyo Suyemoto, "In Topaz," *Trek Literary Magazine* (Topaz, Utah, 1943), WRA Records.
3. Nyogen Sensaki, untitled poem (1945), UCLA.
4. Matsusaburo Hibi, "Speech to Topaz Art School" (1940s), UCLA.
5. Matsusaburo Hibi, "Letter to Cambridge, Mass. Art Exhibit Organizers" (July 28, 1943), UCLA.
6. Anonymous interview (Poston, Ariz., October 12, 1942), Cornell.

That Damned Fence

1. Shizuko Horiuchi, "Letter to Mrs. Henriette B. Von Blon" (Pomona assembly center, Calif., May 24, 1942) in Henriette B. Von Blon Collection (Palo Alto: Hoover Institution Archives).
2. War Relocation Authority Report (1942), WRA Records.
3. Togo Tanaka, quoted in Audrie Girdner and Anne Loftis, *The Great Betrayal* (New York: Macmillan, 1969), p. 238.
4. War Relocation Authority Report (1943), WRA Records.
5. Block Manager's Log (Poston, Ariz., November 12, 1942), Cornell.
6. War Relocation Authority Report (1943), WRA Records.
7. Dies Committee Report, quoted in Girdner and Loftis, p. 298.
8. Dillon Myer, quoted in Girdner and Loftis, p. 298.
9. Unidentified, quoted in Girdner and Loftis, p. 298.
10. Anonymous, "That Damned Fence" (1943), Cornell.

History II: Camp Life

1. Harold Ickes, letter to Franklin D. Roosevelt, April 13, 1943, quoted in Michi Weglyn, *Years of Infamy* (New York: Morrow, 1976), p. 17.

The Sour and the Sweet

1. Ron Wakabayashi, unpublished statement made at the "Day of Remembrance" celebration, Christ United Presbyterian Church, San Francisco, February 19, 1983.
2. Anonymous, "Wrinkles," U.S. War Relocation Authority Papers (Tucson: University of Arizona Library Special Collections).
3. Anonymous journal (June 17, 1943), Cornell.
4. Itsuko Taniguchi, "My Mom, Pop, and Me," Cornell.
5. Poston Junior Red Cross Scrapbook preface (Poston, Ariz., 1940s), Cornell.
6. Michiko Mizumoto, "Manzanar," Cornell.

History III: War Hysteria

1. General John DeWitt, quoted in Dorothy Thomas and Richard Nishimoto, *The Spoilage* (Berkeley: University of California Press, 1969), p. 20.

2. Walter Lippmann, quoted in Frank Chuman, *The Bamboo People: The Law and Japanese Americans* (Del Mar, Calif.: Publishers, Inc., 1976), p. 149.

3. Norman Thomas, quoted in Weglyn, p. 111.

4. Munson Report, quoted in Weglyn, p. 45.

5. John McCloy, quoted in Roger Daniels, *Concentration Camps, North America: Japanese in the United States and Canada during World War II* (Malabar, Fla.: Robert E. Krieger, 1981), p. 65.

You Can't Black Out the Stars

1. Yoshiko Uchida, *Desert Exile: The Uprooting of a Japanese American Family* (Seattle: University of Washington Press, 1982), p. 48.

2. American Friends Service Committee Bulletin (1942) in Conard-Duveneck Collection (Palo Alto: Hoover Institution Archives).

3. Machiye Maxine Nakamura, "How Evacuation Affected Me," in Japanese American War Relocation Collection (Berkeley, Calif.: The Bancroft Library, University of California, Berkeley).

Credits

We thank these organizations and individuals for granting us permission to reproduce paintings and quote from documents in their collections. All other works reproduced are in the possession of the artists or authors identified with them in the text and appear by permission of those persons, to whom we are very grateful.

The Bancroft Library, University of California, Berkeley: from the Japanese American War Relocation Collection: quotations from the essay by Machiye Maxine Nakamura which appear on pp. 26 and 144; the Matsusaburo Hibi woodcut; the Ibuki Hibi drawing.

California First Bank Japanese American History Room, San Francisco: the four paintings by Suiko Mikami.

Cornell University Libraries, Department of Manuscripts and University Archives, Ithaca: from the Japanese American Relocation Center Records: the eleven paintings by Gene Sogioka; also the poems, interviews, and journal entries on pp. 24, 26, 56, 60, 64–65, 90, 91, 94, and 108–9.

Hendrix College, Conway, Arkansas: the Henry Sugimoto painting on p. 36.

Hoover Institution Archives, Stanford University: from the Henriette B. Von Blon Collection: the Shizuko Horiuchi letter quoted on p. 58; from the Conard-Duveneck Collection, the American Friends Service Committee bulletin quoted on p. 142.

University of Arizona Library Special Collections: from the U.S. War Relocation Authority Papers: the poem on pp. 87–88.

University of California, Los Angeles, Department of Special Collections: from the Japanese American Research Project Collection: the Matsusaburo Hibi painting, p. 16, and writings, pp. 23–24 and 52; the poems by Nyogen Sensaki, pp. 18 and 49; the Estelle Ishigo painting, p. 59; and the nine paintings by Kango Takamura.

University of Washington Libraries, Special Collections Division: the drawing by Eddie Sato.

Estate of John Gould Fletcher: the John Gould Fletcher poem on p. 40.

Eiko Katayama: the three paintings by Yonekichi Hosoi.

Mark Luca: the painting on p. 91.

Mrs. Haruko Obata: the eight paintings and the poem by Chiura Obata.

K. Ruth Saito: the Siberius Saito drawing.

Nancy Sato: the two paintings by Yoriyuki Sato.

Mrs. Haruno Tsuruoka: the two paintings by Kakunen Tsuruoka.

Masao Yabuki: the paintings on pp. 92, 93, 95, and 97.

Acknowledgments

We are happy to acknowledge publicly some of the many debts we have incurred in the course of our work. Naturally, without the generosity and cooperation of the artists whose words and paintings appear, this book would still be an idea. Additionally, Virginia Freal, Matsumi Kanemitsu, Mark Luca, Jack Yamasaki, and Taro Yashima increased our understanding of the Japanese American experience during World War II. Although we could not directly incorporate their stories in this book, we thank them for sharing their time with us.

Several Japanese American community groups gave us invaluable assistance in locating artists. In particular, the Japanese American Citizens League's national and regional offices, the Japanese American Cultural and Community Center in Los Angeles, and East Coast Japanese Americans for Redress had a number of fruitful suggestions. A few individuals did most to search their files and jog their memories to help get our project off the ground: Karl Matsushita, library director at the Center for Japanese American Studies in San Francisco; Seizo Oka, vice president at the California First Bank and director of its Japanese American history room in San Francisco; Katsumi Kunitsugu, executive secretary of the Japanese American Cultural and Community Center, Los Angeles; Yoichi Shimatsu, associate producer of a videotape series on the 442nd Regimental Combat Team; Professor Jerrold Takahashi, University of California, Berkeley; and Professor Robert Hosokawa, University of Central Florida. Likewise Dr. Alexander H. Leighton, Dalhousie University, Nova Scotia, Professor Edward Spicer, University of Arizona, and Professor Louis Freund, Hendrix College, Arkansas, answered our many inquiries concerning the relocation and the interned artists with whom they had worked. We are obliged as well to

Don Michelson of Dancer, Fitzgerald, Sample in New York—if he had not located Gene Sogioka, we might never have begun the project—and to Janice Mirikitani and the editors of *Ayumi: A Japanese American Anthology*, which generated many of our initial ideas and proved to be a rich resource. Robert Smith, professor of anthropology at Cornell, provided us with the background we needed to start our project.

Throughout the course of our research, the staffs of the University of Arizona Department of Special Collections, the Bancroft Library at the University of California–Berkeley, the University of California–Los Angeles Department of Special Collections, the Hoover Institution on War, Revolution, and Peace at Stanford University, the Huntington Library in San Marino, the Industrial and Social Branch of the National Archives and Records Service, the University of Utah Department of Special Collections, and the University of Washington Library were efficient, congenial, and otherwise accommodating. Near and dear to our hearts is the staff of the Cornell University Department of Manuscripts and University Archives, whose chairman, H. Thomas Hickerson, went out of his way to support our endeavor.

Our editors at Cornell University Press, Peter Agree and Kay Scheuer especially, we thank for their suggestions and support. Cornell University's Hull Fund made it possible to reproduce all the pictures in color.

J. Victor Koschmann, professor of Japanese history at Cornell University, found time in his incredibly congested schedule to advise our project from its inception. Gould Colman, Cornell University archivist, gave us unmatched guidance at a crucial point in the book's organization. And Richard Polenberg, professor of American history at Cornell, our adviser and friend, more than anyone else provided unwavering support and inspiration. Additionally, all three rigorously critiqued our manuscript. We cannot thank them enough.

Friends and relatives gave us moral support, not to mention food and shelter, in our travels across the country. They are too numerous to mention here; however, those with whom we overstayed our welcome deserve special note: Carin Ashjian, Lilyan, Harry, and Richard Cantor, Jennie Haley, the Karps, the Kronemers, Naomi and Joan Mirman, and Amy Reiff. For services rendered beyond the call of friendship we thank Steve Billmyer, Charlie Goldstein, Dick Horowitz, and from far behind in the seventh inning, the ArcRivals. And finally to our parents, who stood behind us, what can we say?